Death of the Willie Lynch Speech

Exposing the Myth

Death of the Willie Lynch Speech

Exposing the Myth

By Manu Ampim

Death of the Willie Lynch Speech
Exposing the Myth

Published 2013 Black Classic Press

Cover design by Kamau Sennaar
Text design by Charles Lowder

Library of Congress Control Number: 2013934171

ISBN: 978-1-57478-057-4

Printed in the United States of America by BCP Digital Printing, an affiliate of Black Classic Press, Inc.

Due to the dynamic nature of the Internet, any web addresses or links contained in this book may have changed since publication and may no longer be valid.

To review or purchase titles from Black Classic Press, visit: *www.blackclassicbooks.com.*

You may also obtain a list of titles by writing to:
Black Classic Press
c/o List
P.O. Box 13414
Baltimore, MD 21203

Table of Contents

Preface

I first publicly addressed the topic of the Willie Lynch Speech when I gave a presentation on "Primary Research and the Death of Willie Lynch" at the Malonga Casquelourd Center for the Arts on October 27, 2005 as a part of a Maafa Awareness Month event in Oakland, California.

I was invited to participate in a panel discussion on the topic, "Addressing the Residual Psychological Affects of Enslavement: How Does One Heal the Trauma?" Weeks before the event, there was much discussion about the topic and the invited panelists.

My name had been mentioned by several people, but I was not very interested in participating in the panel because too often Black people get stuck on what happened centuries ago as an excuse to not move forward and solve contemporary problems.

When I was contacted about my participation, I raised my concerns about the event not being productive and there being too many panelists to have a discussion of the topic and still have time for a meaningful dialogue with the audience in a short two-hour period. However, I eventually received a phone call from the main organizer Wanda Sabir and agreed to participate after she assured me that the event would focus on practical solutions and that there would be fewer panelists than there had been the previous year.

I decided that since the community wanted me to participate, I should make sure that my involvement would make an impact for the ages. As a result, I started brainstorming about a well-known topic that I could present that would challenge a popular belief. After a short while, it became clear that the most appropriate topic would be for me to attack the popular "Willie Lynch" myth.

I had always dismissed this fake "Willie Lynch" speech as a kindergarten attempt to "wake up" Black people to the effects of slavery in the U.S., but this was now a perfect opportunity to address this popular myth once and for all and effectively present my case that the so-called "Willie Lynch Letter" was a 20th century fake. For my remarks, I gave a Powerpoint presentation on "Primary Research and the Death of Willie Lynch." I began my presentation by stating that my goal was to reverse the thinking of many people by destroying a popular myth.

Immediately after the panel concluded, a number of people approached me in shock that "Willie Lynch" was a modern myth, and they were inspired to inform others to stop promoting the fake speech. Soon afterwards, I was invited to publish an essay, "Death of the Willie Lynch Speech," in the winter 2005/2006 issue of *Nex Generation Magazine* (London, England).

Then I wrote part two of this essay for the spring 2006 issue of the magazine and later posted both essays on my website. Since these events, my "Death of the Willie Lynch Speech" essays have gone viral on the internet, taking on a life of their own far beyond what I had ever expected.

When the opportunity presented itself again to publish these essays together in a common context, I welcomed the occasion to share the additional insights that I've gained on this topic since they were originally published. I received countless email messages, letters, and phone calls in response to my essays. The most interesting email that I received was from the alleged forger of the original Willie Lynch Speech after he read my first essay online, and his entire confession letter is included in Appendix I. I have also compiled a selection of the other email messages in Appendix II.

And so the dialogue and subsequent debate continue about the authenticity and accuracy of the so-called Willie Lynch Speech. For my part, I continue to dispel the myth of secret documents and "slave consultants." As a professional historian and primary researcher, my work is to help destroy misinformation and continue teaching the public about the authentic past in order to examine and solve contemporary problems in the African American community.

—Professor Manu Ampim
Oakland, California
July 2012

Death of the Willie Lynch Speech (Part I)

Author's Note: This essay was first published in the winter 2005/2006 issue of Nex Generation Magazine (London, England). Editor Brother Dekenu invited me to submit the essay as a way to help dispel the "Willie Lynch" myth in the United Kingdom.

A year earlier in October 2004, Dekenu had invited me to London to give a week-long series of presentations and workshops on primary research methods and Africana Studies. The presentations were a success, and we both felt that an analysis of the "Death of the Willie Lynch Speech" essay was a good follow-up example of the power of primary research as a weapon against the distortion of African American history.

Since 1995 there has been much attention given to a speech claimed to be delivered by a "William Lynch" in 1712. This speech has been promoted widely throughout African American and Black British circles. It is re-printed on numerous websites, discussed in chat rooms, forwarded as a "did you know" email to friends and family members, assigned as required readings in college and high school courses, promoted at conferences, and there are several books published with the title of "Willie Lynch."[1] In addition, new terminology called the "Willie Lynch Syndrome" has been devised to explain the psychological problems and the disunity among Black people.

Further, it is naively assumed by a large number of Willie Lynch believers that this single and isolated speech, allegedly given almost 300 years ago, completely explains the internal problems and divisions within the African American community. They assume that the "Willie Lynch Syndrome" explains Black disunity and the psychological trauma of slavery. While some have questioned and even dismissed this speech from the outset, it is fair to say that most African Americans who are aware of the speech have not questioned its authenticity and assume it to be a legitimate and very crucial historical document that explains what has happened to African Americans.

However, when we examine the details of the "Willie Lynch Speech" and its assumed influence, then it becomes clear that the belief in its authenticity and widespread adoption during the slavery era is nothing more than a modern myth. In this brief examination, I will show that the only known "William Lynch" was born three decades after the alleged speech, that the only known "William Lynch" did not own a plantation in the West Indies, that the "speech" was not mentioned by *anyone* in the 18th or 19th centuries, and that the "speech" itself clearly indicates that it was composed in the late 20th century.

Silence on the Lynch Speech

The "Willie Lynch Speech" is not mentioned by *any* 18th or 19th century slave masters or anti-slavery activists. There is a large body of written materials from the slavery era; yet there is not one reference to a William Lynch speech given in 1712. This is very curious because both free and enslaved African Americans wrote and spoke about the tactics and practices of white slave masters. Frederick Douglass, Nat Turner, Olaudah Equino, David Walker, Maria Stewart, Martin Delaney, Henry Highland Garnet, Richard Allen, Absolom Jones, Frances Harper, William Wells Brown, and Robert Purvis were African Americans who initiated various efforts to rise up against the slave system; yet none cited the alleged Lynch speech. Also, there is not a single reference to the Lynch speech by any white abolitionists, including John Brown, William Lloyd Garrison, and Wendell Phillips. Similarly, there has been no evidence found of slave masters or pro-slavery advocates referring to (not to mention utilizing) the specific divide and rule information given in the Lynch speech.

Likewise, none of the most credible historians on the enslavement of African Americans have ever mentioned the Lynch speech in any of their writings. A reference to the Lynch speech, and its alleged divide and rule tactics, is completely missing in the works of Benjamin Quarles, John Hope Franklin, John Henrik Clarke, W.E.B. Du Bois, Herbert Aptheker, Kenneth Stampp, John Blassingame, Rosalyn Terborg-Penn, Darlene Clark-Hine, and Lerone Bennett. These authors have studied the details and dynamics of Black social life and relations during slavery, as well as the "machinery of control" by the slave masters; yet none made a single reference to a Lynch speech.

Since the Willie Lynch speech was not mentioned by any slave masters, pro-slavery advocates, abolitionists, or historians studying the slavery era, the question of course is when did it appear?

First Reference to the Lynch Speech

The first reference to the Willie Lynch speech was in a late 1993 online listing of sources posted by Anne Taylor, who was then the reference librarian at the University of Missouri at St. Louis (UMSL).[2] She posted ten sources to the UMSL library database, and the Lynch speech was the last item in the listing. In her 1995 email exchanges with the late Dr. William Piersen (Professor of History, Fisk University) and others interested in the origin of the Lynch speech, Taylor indicated that she kept the source from where she received the speech anonymous upon request because he was unable to establish the authenticity of the document. On October 31, 1995, Taylor wrote:

"Enough butt-covering, now it's time to talk about where I got it. The publisher who gave me this [speech] wanted to remain anonymous…because he couldn't trace it, either, and until now I've honored his wishes. It was printed in a local, widely-distributed, free publication called *The St. Louis Black Pages*, 9th anniversary edition, 1994*, page 8."

[*Taylor notes: "At risk of talking down to you, it's not unusual for printed materials to be 'post-dated'– the 1994 edition came out in 1993]. [3]

The Lynch speech was distributed in the Black community in 1993 and 1994, and in fact I came across it during this time period or maybe a few years earlier. However, as an historian trained in Africana Studies and primary research, I never took it seriously. I simply read it and put it in a file somewhere.

However, the Lynch speech was popularized at the Million Man March (held in Washington, DC) on October 16, 1995, when it was referred to by Min. Louis Farrakhan. He stated:

> *We, as a people who have been fractured, divided and destroyed because of our division, now must move toward a perfect union. Let's look at a speech, delivered by a white slave holder on the banks of the James River in 1712… Listen to what he said. He said, 'In my bag, I have a foolproof method of controlling Black slaves. I guarantee every one of you, if installed correctly, it will control the slaves for at least 300 years'… So spoke Willie Lynch 283 years ago.*

The 1995 Million Man March was broadcasted live on C-Span television, and thus millions of people throughout the U.S. and the world heard about the alleged Willie Lynch speech for the first time. Now, ten years later, the speech has become extremely popular although many historians and critical thinkers questioned this strange and unique document from the outset.

Full Text of the Willie Lynch Speech (Supposedly Given in 1712)

Gentlemen, I greet you here on the bank of the James River in the year of our Lord one thousand seven hundred and twelve. First, I shall thank you, the gentlemen of the Colony of Virginia, for bringing me here. I am here to help you solve some of your problems with slaves. Your invitation reached me on my modest plantation in the West Indies where I have experimented with some of the newest and still the oldest methods of control of slaves.

Ancient Rome would envy us if my program were implemented. As our boat sailed south on the James River, named for our illustrious King, whose version of the Bible we cherish. I saw enough to know that your problem is not unique. While Rome used cords of woods as crosses for standing human bodies along its highways in great numbers you are here using the tree and the rope on occasion.

I caught the whiff of a dead slave hanging from a tree a couple of miles back. You are not only losing a valuable stock by hangings, you are having uprisings, slaves are running away, your crops are sometimes left in the fields too long for maximum profit, you suffer occasional fires, [and] your animals are killed.

Gentlemen, you know what your problems are: I do not need to elaborate. I am not here to enumerate your problems. I am here to introduce you to a method of solving them. In my bag here, I have a fool proof method for controlling your Black slaves. I guarantee every one of you that if installed correctly it will control the slaves for at least 300 hundred years [sic]. My method is simple. Any member of your family or your overseer can use it.

I have outlined a number of differences among the slaves: and I take these differences and make them bigger. I use fear, distrust, and envy for control purposes. These methods have worked on my modest plantation in the West Indies and it will work throughout the South. Take this simple little list of differences, and think about them.

On top of my list is 'Age', but it is there only because it starts with an 'A': the second is 'Color' or shade, there is intelligence, size, sex, size of plantations, status on plantation, attitude of owners, whether the slave lived in the valley, on hill, East, West, North, South, have fine hair, coarse hair, or is tall or short. Now that you have a list of differences, I shall give you an outline of action–but before that I shall assure you that distrust is stronger than trust and envy is stronger than adulation, respect, or admiration.

The Black slave after receiving this indoctrination shall carry on and will become self re-fueling and self generating for hundreds of years, maybe thousands. Don't forget you must pitch the old Black male vs. the young Black male, and the young Black male against the old Black male. You must use the dark skin slaves vs. the light skin slaves and the light skin slaves vs. the dark skin slaves. You must use the female vs. the male, and the male vs. the female. You must also have your white servants and overseers distrust all Blacks, but it is necessary that your slaves trust and depend on us. They must love, respect and trust only us.

Gentlemen, these kits are your keys to control. Use them. Have your wives and children use them, never miss an opportunity. If used intensely for one year, the slaves themselves will remain perpetually distrustful. Thank you, gentlemen.

Who Was "Willie Lynch"?

The only known "William Lynch" who could have authorized a 1712 speech in Virginia was born 30 years *after* the alleged speech was given. The only known "William Lynch" lived from 1742-1820 and was from Pittsylvania, Virginia. It is obvious that "William Lynch" could not have authored a document 30 years before he was born! This "William Lynch" never owned a plantation in the West Indies, and he did not own a slave plantation in Virginia.

Divide and Rule

The Lynch speech lists a number of *divide and rule* tactics that were not important concerns to slaveholders in the early 1700s, and they certainly were not adopted. The anonymous writer of the Lynch speech states, "I have outlined a number of differences among the slaves, and I take these differences and make them bigger." Here is the list provided in the Lynch speech: age, color, intelligence, fine hair vs. coarse hair, tall vs. short, and male vs. female.

However, none of these "tactics" were concerns to slaveholders in the early 1700s in the West Indies or colonial America. No credible historian has indicated that any of the items on the Lynch list were a part of a *divide and rule* strategy in the early 18th century. These are current 20th century divisions and concerns. Here are the Lynch speech tactics versus the real *divide and rule* tactics that were actually used in the early 18th century:

Lynch Speech Tactics	**Real Divide and Rule Tactics**
Age	Ethnic origin and language
Color (light vs. dark skin)	African born vs. American born
Intelligence	Occupation (house vs. field slave)
Fine hair vs. coarse hair	Reward system for "good" behavior
Tall vs. short	Class status
Male vs. female	Outlawed social gatherings

It is certain that "Willie Lynch" did not use his divide and rule tactics on his "modest plantation in the West Indies."

20th Century Terms in the Lynch Speech

There are a number of terms in the alleged 1712 Lynch speech that are undoubtedly *anachronisms* (i.e. words that are out of their proper historical time period). Here are a few of the words in the speech that were not used until the 20th century:

Lynch speech: "In my bag here, I have a **fool-proof** method for controlling your **Black** slaves."

Anachronisms: "Fool proof" and "Black" with an upper-case "B" to refer to people of African descent are of 20th century origin. Capitalizing "Black" did not become a standard form of writing until the late 1960s.

Lynch speech: "The Black slave after receiving this indoctrination shall carry on and will become **self re-fueling** and self generating for hundreds of years."

Anachronism: "Re-fueling" is a 20th century term which refers to transportation.

Other Strange Features

• William Lynch is invited from the "West Indies" (with no specific country indicated) to give only a short eight-paragraph speech. The cost of such a trip would have been considerable, and for the invited speaker to give only general remarks would have been highly unlikely.

• Lynch never thanked the specific host of his speech. He only thanked "the gentlemen of the Colony of Virginia, for bringing me here." Here, he is rude and shows a lack of etiquette. Also, no specific *location* for the speech was stated, only that he was speaking "on the bank [sic] of the James River."

• Lynch claims that on his journey to give the speech he saw "a dead slave hanging from a tree." This is highly unlikely because lynching African Americans from trees did not become common until the late 19th century.

• Lynch claims that his method of control will work for "at least 300 hundred years [sic]." First, it has gone unnoticed that the modern writer of the "speech" wrote three hundred twice ("300 hundred years"), which makes no grammatical sense. It should be "300 years" or "three hundred years." Second, the arbitrary choice of 300 years is interesting because it happens to conveniently bring us to the present time.

• Lynch claims that his method of control "will work throughout the *South.*" This statement clearly shows the modern writer's historical ignorance. In 1712, there was no region in the current-day U.S. identified as the "South."The geographical region of the "South" did not become distinct until a century after the alleged speech. Before the American Revolutionary War vs. Britain (1775-1783), the 13 original U.S. colonies were *all* slaveholding regions, and most of these colonies were in what later became the North, not the "South." In fact, the region with the second largest slave population during the time of the alleged William Lynch speech was the northern city of New York where there were a significant number of slave revolts including the rebellion in 1712.

• Lynch fails to give "an outline of action" for control as he promised in his speech. He only gives a "simple little list of differences" among "Black slaves."

• Lynch lists his differences in alphabetical order. He states: "On top of my list is 'Age', but it is there only because it starts with an 'A'." Yet, after the first two differences ("age" and "color"), Lynch's list is anything but alphabetical.

• Lynch spells "color" in the American form instead of the British form ("colour"). We are led to believe that Lynch was a British slave owner in the "West Indies;" yet he does not write in British style.

• Lastly, the name *Willie Lynch* is interesting as it may be a simple play on words: "Will Lynch" or "Will he Lynch." This may be a modern psychological game being played on unsuspecting believers.

Who Wrote the Lynch Speech?

It is clear that the "Willie Lynch Speech" is a late 20th century invention because of the numerous reasons outlined in this essay. I would advance that the likely candidate for such a superficial speech is an African American male in the 20s-30s age range, who probably minored in Black Studies in college. He had a limited knowledge of 18th century America, but unfortunately he fooled many uncritical Black people.

Some people argue that it doesn't matter if the speech is fact or fiction because white people did use tactics to divide us. Of course tactics were used, but what advocates of this argument don't understand is that African people will not solve our problems and address the real issues confronting us by adopting half-baked urban myths. If there are people who know that the Lynch speech is fictional, but continue to promote it in order to "wake us up," then we should be very suspicious of these people, who lack integrity and will openly violate trust and willingly lie to our community.

Even if the Willie Lynch mythology were true, the speech is focused on *what white slaveholders were doing, and there is no plan, program, or any agenda items for Black people to implement.* It is ludicrous to give god-like powers to one white man who allegedly gave a single speech almost 300 years ago and claim that this is the main reason why Black people have problems among us today. Unfortunately, too often Black people would rather believe a simple and convenient myth rather than spend the time studying and understanding a situation. Too many of our people want a one-page, simplified Ripley's Believe It or Not explanation of "what happened."

Willie Lynch Distraction

While we are distracted by the Willie Lynch urban mythology, the real issues go ignored. There are a number of authentic first-hand written accounts by enslaved Africans, who wrote specifically about the slave conditions and the slave masters' system of control. For example, writers such as Olaudah Equiano, Mahommah Baquaqua, and Frederick Douglass wrote penetrating accounts about the tactics of slave control.

Frederick Douglass, for instance, wrote in his autobiography, *Narrative of the life of Frederick Douglass,* that one of the most diabolical tactics of the American slaveholders was to force the slave workers during their six days off for the Christmas holiday to drink themselves into a drunken stupor and forget about the pain of slavery. Douglass wrote, "It was deemed a disgrace not to get drunk at Christmas; and he was regarded as lazy indeed, who had not provided himself with the necessary means, during the year, to get whiskey enough to last him through Christmas. From what I know of the effects of these holidays upon the slave, I believe them to be the most effective means in the hands of the slaveholder in keeping down the spirit of insurrection. Were the slaveholders at once to abandon this practice, I have not the slightest doubt it would lead to an immediate insurrection among the slaves.... The holidays are part and parcel of the gross fraud, wrong, and inhumanity of slavery." [4]

Also, many nineteenth-century Black writers discussed the specific tactics of the white slave owners and how they used Christianity to teach the enslaved Africans how to be docile and accept their slave status. The problem with African American and Black British revelry during the Christmas holidays and the blind acceptance of the master's version of Christianity are no doubt major issues among Black people today. It is certain that both of these problems were initiated and perpetuated during slavery, and they require our immediate attention.

Many people who embrace the Willie Lynch myth have not studied that period of slavery and have not read the major works or first-hand documents on this issue of African American slavery. Further, as indicated above, the Lynch hoax is so widespread that this fictional speech is amazingly used as required reading by some college instructors. While we are being misled by this fantasy, the real historical data is being ignored. For example, Kenneth Stampp in his important work on slavery in the American South, *The Peculiar Institution* (1956), uses historical records to outline the five rules for making a slave:

1. Maintain strict discipline.
2. Instill belief of personal inferiority.
3. Develop awe of master's power (instill fear).
4. Accept master's standards of "good conduct."
5. Develop a habit of perfect dependence.[5]

Primary (first-hand) research is the most effective weapon against the distortion of African American history and culture. *Primary research* training is the best defense against urban legends and modern myths. It is now time for critical thinkers to bury the decade-old mythology of "William Lynch."

NOTES

1. For example, see: Lawanda Staten, *How to Kill Your Willie Lynch* (1997); Kashif Malik Hassan-el, *The Willie Lynch Letter and the Making of a Slave* (1999); Marc Sims, *Willie Lynch: Why African-Americans Have So Many Issues!* (2002); Alvin Morrow, *Breaking the Curse of Willie Lynch* (2003); and *Slave Chronicles, The Willie Lynch Letter and the Destruction of Black Unity* (2004).

2. See:
www.umsl.edu/services/library/blackstudies/narrate.htm

3. For this quote and the general Anne Taylor email exchanges regarding the authenticity of the Willie Lynch speech, see: www.umsl.edu/services/library/blackstudies/winbail.htm

4. Frederick Douglass, *Narrative of the Life of Frederick Douglass* (1845), p. 84.

5. Kenneth Stampp, *The Peculiar Institution: Slavery in the Ante-Bellum South* (1956), pp. 144-48.

Death of the Willie Lynch Speech (Part II)

Author's Note: *The first "Death of the Willie Lynch Speech" essay received widespread attention throughout the United Kingdom, United States, and Canada. It went viral online and is discussed in college classrooms throughout the U.S. Thus, I decided to write this second piece to summarize the numerous responses to the first essay and explain the source of many contemporary African American problems. It was first published in the spring 2006 issue of Nex Generation Magazine (London, England).*

Responses to Part I

Since my first essay on the fictional "Willie Lynch" speech in the previous issue of *Nex Generation,* there has been an overwhelming response to my analysis of this prevailing myth among Black people in the Western hemisphere.

There have been three main responses to my "Willie Lynch" essay, and 90 percent of these responses fall into the first two groups (See Appendix II for a selection of these email responses).

The first group of responses is from those people who were very thankful to read my work because they knew the Willie Lynch speech was a fake, but they had no real proof. Before reading the evidence presented in my essay, this group either ignored this fake speech, or they argued against its authenticity without the ammunition that my critique provides.

The second group of people also responded to my essay very favorably. However, this group initially assumed that the alleged speech was authentic and thus shared it with many people in their networks. They simply never thought to ask themselves whether the speech was legitimate. Since reading my analysis of the Lynch speech, this group now sees it as a modern hoax and has indicated that they are going back to their networks to announce that the Willie Lynch speech is a modern fake. I have the utmost respect for the people in this group because they have a high degree of integrity to admit that they had made a mistake and were now going back to make corrections.

The final group represents about 10 percent of the responses to my Lynch essay, and most of these people suffer from a complete lack of critical thinking skills. Many of them claim, "Even if the speech is a fake, it is still true!" Their position is essentially that "the speech is important to me, and I don't care that it is probably fake; I still believe it is true." Some of these people have stated that they go so far as to meditate on the speech every day or every week. This group vows to continue referencing the Willie Lynch speech because they believe it to be an important 'wake up" call for Black people. However, they fail to realize that the fake speech is only concerned with what a white slave-owner supposedly said, and there is no agenda or program for Black people to act upon. Also, they fail to understand that few people would consider trusting someone who they know will openly lie when it serves their interests.

In fact, a more dramatic "wake-up" call for Black people than the fake Lynch speech was the 1977 TV miniseries "Roots." Roots graphically introduced millions of viewers throughout the world to the brutality of American slavery, and yet this powerful "wake up" call didn't help us to solve any of our major problems. In fact, today one-third of Black children in America still live in poverty, and since the Roots miniseries, there are now more African American men in prison than there are in college. Lastly, there are some people in this 10-percent group who have a particular interest in promoting the Lynch myth because they want an excuse to continue sitting on their behinds and doing nothing to help solve problems in our communities. They claim that Willie Lynch (who they promote as a powerful white god) gave a single speech 300 years ago, and this is why Black people can't come together to solve our problems today.

If the Willie Lynch speech supporters are sincere and want to learn about influential and prominent pro-slavery advocates in the 1700s and 1800s, then they should read the recent book by Paul Finkelman, *Defending Slavery: Proslavery Thought in the Old South (A Brief History with Documents)* (2003). Of course, of all the most influential people noted in this study, neither "Willie Lynch" nor his alleged speech is mentioned in this work.

Negative Effects of the 20th Century

As I indicated in Part I, there is absolutely no record of a 1712 Willie Lynch speech or any of the Lynch tactics being used in the 18th century or referred to by any historians, pro-slavery advocates, or anti-slavery abolitionists in the 18th or 19th century. There is no doubt that the fake Lynch document is of late 20th century origin and thus far it cannot be conclusively traced back before 1993. The problem with believing silly internet fairy tales is that if we don't know the origin of a problem, then it is impossible to create a solution because the ideas are based on false information. Black people will never be respected as an intelligent people or solve any of our major problems by believing in kindergarten internet myths.

Many of the problems that Black people are facing today developed in the 20th century during and after the great African American migrations around World War I and World War II. When we actually look at the negative effects of these *migrations, urbanization, and later integration,* then it becomes clear that many of the problems that we are faced with today have no direct connection to slavery (even though slavery was a vicious institution). Rather, these problems arose as Black people migrated from the southern region of the U.S. in the 20th century and lost the connection to our cultural values. It is well known that the social harmony within the African American community still existed well into the 20th century. In fact, all older Black people from the South know this from their own experience and the experience of their parents and grandparents, as there were largely positive marriage and family relations, respect for eldership, and general social harmony.

Yet, many people ignore this fact of Black social harmony in the early-to mid-20th century in order to believe the Willie Lynch fairy tale. This fake speech is a serious distraction because rather than addressing the real sources of our problems, many people continue to falsely believe that "everything" comes from slavery and that "Willie Lynch" was a white god who gave a single speech that somehow controls 40 million Black people 300 years later.

As I indicated in my first essay, there are many first-hand slavery accounts that give more important insight as to what happened to Black people than the fake Willie Lynch speech. In order to gain correct knowledge of our historical experience, we have to study our history from the primary sources and study the works of professional sociologists and historians such as Benjamin Quarles, Carter G. Woodson, W.E.B. Du Bois, John Blassingame, Eugene Genovese, Herbert Gutman, and Robert Staples. These authors clearly demonstrate that African American social harmony survived throughout slavery and into the 20th century. The Black political and cultural resistance to enslavement never ceased and indeed prevented the forces of slavery from destroying the Black sense of community sharing and caring as is falsely asserted by the dwindling number of Lynch speech supporters.

In the early 20th century, there was a fundamental shift that occurred in the situation of African Americans when for the first time, there was a major migration of Black people away from the southern U.S. during and after World War I (1914-1918). Before this great migration, 90 percent of African Americans lived in the South. According to the U.S. census figures between 1910-1920, there were several hundred thousand Black people who left the South searching for a better way of life and migrated to northern cities such as New York, Chicago, Philadelphia, Detroit, St. Louis, Cleveland, Pittsburgh, Gary, and Columbus and Akron, Ohio. These northern cities were dramatically transformed within one to two generations into areas which housed growing impoverished Black populations.

These Black migrants had to squeeze into low-rent districts in the inner-cities, which eventually turned into Black slums. The Black migrants left their southern rural problems only to be met with a new set of urban problems in northern (and southern) cities, which were anything but "a land of promise" as many of them had hoped. There were racial tensions with white citizens in these cities, who did not welcome this wave of Black immigrants. Whites feared that this new Black presence would ruin their neighborhoods and take their jobs. As a result, white mobs instigated race riots in numerous cities during this era, most notably in East St. Louis (1917), Houston (1917), Chicago (1919), Elaine, Arkansas (1919), Tulsa, Oklahoma (1921), and Rosewood, Florida (1923).

The second major 20th century migration was during and after World War II (1939-1945). There was a massive wave of African Americans who again left the southern U.S., but this time they migrated to the western U.S. cities in California and elsewhere. Thus in 1910, African Americans were predominantly rural and southern; approximately 75 percent lived in rural areas, and 90 percent lived in the South. A half-century later African Americans were mainly an urban population, as almost three-fourths of them lived in cities. Within a few decades after the first migration, many northern cities were transformed into Black slum areas. In addition, the introduction of drugs into inner-city urban communities by U.S. government forces also had a devastating impact on Black life. For an example, see *Dark Alliance: The CIA, the Contras, and the Crack Cocaine Explosion* by Gary Webb (1999).

Although both the *migrations* and the *urbanization* had a negative impact on black life and social harmony, which existed in the southern rural communities, it was the third major factor of *integration* that caused the greatest rift among African Americans. After the pivotal 1954 Brown vs. Board of Education decision, which outlawed the Jim Crow racial segregation in U.S. public schools, Black people began to attend all-white schools, learn white values, live in white neighborhoods, and spend money in white stores. Integration dealt a devastating blow to Black unity and sense of community. During a February 2006 presentation at Merritt College (Oakland, Calif.), Dr. Oba T'Shaka mentioned the main premise of his book *Integration Trap, Generation Gap:* There have been more divisions among Black people since 1968 than there were during the entire period of more than three hundred years from 1619 to 1968. He argues that integration has been nothing more than a trap to destroy Black unity.

There is no question that since the late 1960s and early 1970s Black people have suffered from the loss of independent schools and businesses and have faced the onslaught of street gangs, crack-cocaine, homicides, the incarceration of young Black men, a high divorce rate and single-parent households, the rape of women, and the disrespect of elders, etc. None of these problems were significant issues before the 20th century *migrations, urbanization,* and the *integration* trap. In the early 20th century, Black social harmony was a basic reality, and caring and sharing were fundamental characteristics of virtually every Black community. The greatest issue for Black people has been the loss of the African-centered system of ethics and values, which linked Black people together and allowed us to survive the vicious system of slavery and later Jim Crow (characterized by racial segregation and anti-Black violence).

Future of the "Lynch Speech"

If we study the origins of the negative factors of *migrations, urbanization,* and *integration,* then we will not only understand how problems developed among African Americans in the 20th century, but of course there would be no need for misinformed people to continue promoting a fake speech given by a mythical slave owner.

The death of the "Willie Lynch speech" is imminent as more people see through the superficial attempt to "wake up" Black people with a fake document while ignoring the real sources of Black problems. The internet has undoubtedly been the main avenue to spread false information, and some have made money by promoting their Lynch books and speeches, but it is the minority of college instructors who should also be questioned for misleading students with the bogus Lynch "document." Rather than introducing students to first-hand sources and teaching them critical thinking skills, these instructors are contributing to the spread of ignorance. However, these instructors should be on notice that many of their students now doubt what they have learned in their classes because they realize that they have already been misled to believe in a modern internet hoax.

In the arena of serious scholarship and primary (first-hand) research, the standing rule is that *"documentation beats conversation."* There is a fundamental difference between proof and propaganda, between evidence and ideology, and between knowledge and mere belief. In the next five years, the Lynch speech will likely be a forgotten myth of the past.

Death of the Willie Lynch Speech (Part III)

12 Reasons to Stop Promoting the Fake "Willie Lynch" Speech

Author's Note: *Although the first two essays were widely read, discussed, and debated by a number of people from the end of 2005 to early 2010, I thought that my main contribution to dispelling the Willie Lynch myth was over. However in February 2010, I spoke with the individual who purports to have concocted the fake Lynch speech in 1979, and as a result, I immediately drafted part III of this essay as a way of documenting my thoughts, although I never published them (see Appendix I for details).*

Later, in early 2011, the editors of Ourstory Journal (Detroit, MI) contacted me and asked me to offer any materials that I had written on the "Willie Lynch" myth. Consequently I submitted part III of this series. All three essays were published in the Ourstory Journal (Summer 2011, volume 1, number 2).

It is well-documented that slavery was a brutal anti-Black institution organized by Euro-Americans, and thus there is no reason to add silly myths to this fact. However, many people are lazy and do not want to research and read important works on slavery. They want a *Ripley's Believe It or Not* version of history that summarizes the entire 400-year experience of Black people in one page. Even the alleged forger of the Willie Lynch "document" (see #2 below) has stated that the speech "will not show you how to control a population, you have to go deeper" than this.

1. No one has ever found an original copy of the "Willie Lynch" speech. Likewise, in the longer version of the fake Lynch speech, Frederick Douglass' name is mentioned as the author, but the 20th century fabricator never considered the fact that the *Douglass Papers* are in the Library of Congress (Washington, DC), and there is no such document related to "Willie Lynch" in these files. This can be verified by either visiting the Library of Congress or searching the files online (www.loc.gov). As I documented in Part I, the fake Lynch "document" first appeared in an online database in 1993. The person who gave the "document" to the librarian, who posted it online at the University of Missouri at St. Louis, asked to remain anonymous. *Authentic* documents do not just magically appear in a cloud of secrecy.

2. Since my writing of the first two Willie Lynch essays, the man who claims to have created the *first version* of the fake Willie Lynch "speech" contacted me to confess his actions. The forger wrote a confession letter to me to indicate that he fabricated the "speech" in 1979 and he willingly, but reluctantly, admitted his actions to me because I pinpointed the profile of the person who wrote the modern speech. In Part I, I stated the following, "It is clear that the 'Willie Lynch Speech' is a late 20th century invention because of the numerous reasons outlined in this essay. I would advance that the likely candidate for such a superficial speech is an African American male in the 20s-30s age range, who probably minored in Black Studies in college. He had a limited knowledge of 18th century America, but unfortunately he fooled many uncritical Black people." When the forger read my comments while he was surfing the net, he indicated that he simply said, "Damn, the brother got me!" because of my accurate description.

In my next communication, I will give the full details of the forger's identity and his confession statement, but he asked that I not reveal his name until he finishes his next book. I will respect his request and give him a short amount of time before presenting all of the details of this entire story. Suffice it to say that the alleged forger is an established faculty member of a noted university, he has a Ph.D. in psychology and specializes in brainwashing, and he is a long-time member of a Black psychological group.

3. There has been complete silence from all of the noted historians, anti-slavery abolitionists, and pro-slavery advocates alike regarding the "slave consultant" Willie Lynch or his alleged 1712 speech. There is not a single mention of this alleged consultant or his influential "speech." (Many Willie Lynch followers incorrectly state that it was a "letter" that he wrote instead of a speech he gave).

4. There are many who know (and admit) that the "speech" is fake, but they want to "wake up" Black people. In other words, they consciously lie to Black people when it is convenient. What else are these people willing to lie to us about if it serves their interest? Besides, the racism (white supremacy) and lack of response in the wake of Hurricane Katrina (2005) and the flooding of New Orleans is the biggest "wake up" call that any of us has seen in the 21st century. Never before have we witnessed an entire urban Black population permanently dislocated from a modern U.S. city.

Black people have had many real life wake-up calls in America, and the Willie Lynch supporters can take their pick of the shocking real life historical speeches, documents, and events that have "woken up" the Black community. They could choose from this list if they are short on historical facts: David Walker, *Appeal to the Coloured Citizens of the World* (1829); Henry Highland Garnet, "An Address to the Slaves of the United States" (1843); William Wells Brown, "Slavery As it Is" (1847);

Frederick Douglass' "What to the Slave Is the 4th of July" (1852); Paul Finkleman, *Defending Slavery: Proslavery Thought in the Old South (A Brief History with Documents)*, 2003; James Allen, *Without Sanctuary: Lynching Photography in America (2000);* Frances Cress Welsing, *The Cress Theory of Color Confrontation and Racism /White Supremacy* (1989); Cheikh Anta Diop's "Two Cradle Theory" in *The Cultural Unity of Black Africa* (2000); Michael Bradley, *Iceman Inheritance* (1991); the assassination of Black leaders in the 1960s; and the 1991 videotaped beating of Rodney King.

5. Since the publication of my first two essays in this series, the argument has shifted from the Willie Lynch speech being "real" to the position that "the speech may be a myth, but the tactics outlined in the speech were real." The major problem with this position is that the tactics outlined in the Lynch speech were not used by slave masters. There is no evidence that there was any system by which slave masters divided Black people based on male vs. female, young vs. old, or tall vs. short, etc. The Lynch promoters have no concern for the fact that these are late 20th century issues.

The actual historical tools of control were to use violence, instill fear, and force Black people to adopt the slave master's values and belief system to keep them subservient and docile. The specific tactics that were used are clearly documented in the first-hand texts of Frederick Douglass, David Walker, Olaudah Equino, and others. These tactics included division by language, ethnicity, occupation, or class status. Also, Paul Finkleman's work, *Defending Slavery* (2003), contains the most influential first-hand documents used and promoted in the 18th and 19th centuries by the defenders of slavery, and there is no mention of Willie Lynch and his alleged "tactics."

6. The information in the 1712 "Willie Lynch speech" is false and based on historical ignorance. Here are a few facts: (1) In 1712 Queen Anne was the ruler of England, and King James I (1566-1625) had long been dead for almost a century. In this 100-year period, there were no less than six rulers of England since the time between James and the alleged speech, and very few people would have still seen James as an "illustrious king." By comparison, as proud as many people are to be "American," very few of them have any idea who was a U.S. president 100 years ago. (2) Hanging Black people from trees was a practice that began in the mid-1800s and was not a method of murder used in 1712. (3) The term "Black" as an ethnic indicator with a capital "B" was not used in the 18th century. The capitalized term "Black" did not come into usage until the emergence of the Black Power Movement in June 1966. (4) There was no such region as the "South" in 1712. This regional designation did not occur until after the American Revolutionary War (1775-1783). Before this time there was simply the "13 American colonies" without any distinction between "North" and "South." (5) If Willie Lynch was a slave owner of British descent, he would have certainly used the British spelling of "colour" (instead of "color").

7. "Willie Lynch" and white people are not omnipotent gods with the power to make a single speech and somehow control 40 million Black people 300 years later. Black people should leave the cult and stop worshipping Willie Lynch and the powers of white people because they are not gods.

8. The fake Lynch speech keeps Black people in a mode of ignorance where they believe in "Ripley's Believe It Or Not" kindergarten myths. Rather than learning critical thinking skills and accessing primary sources to learn about their history, the

Willie Lynch cult followers are more focused on promoting urban myths. This cult following keeps Black people in the perpetual role of simple-minded people who are constant victims focused on their victimization and can do nothing because Willie Lynch has such omnipotent authority.

The use of a fictional kindergarten "document" instead of original first-hand materials is completely unnecessary and teaches Black people to believe in fairy tale myths rather than learning legitimate research methods. The Willie Lynch fairy tale has no more historical value in the progress of African Americans than the Easter Bunny, the Tooth Fairy, Mary Poppins, or Santa Claus.

9. Even if the fake "Willie Lynch" speech were a legitimate document, it does not give Black people anything to do. There is no agenda or plan of action except to be in awe of Willie Lynch's power. Like most urban legends, the Lynch speech is simply designed to create shock without outlining any plan of action. Black people are presented as helpless victims, who are hopelessly paralyzed by a 300-year old speech and unable to solve social problems because of Lynch's mighty authority. This is a perfect excuse for the lazy person who has no real interest in working to solve the problems in the African American community.

10. Knowledge of the "Willie Lynch speech" has done absolutely nothing to improve the material conditions of Black people in America. It has not improved marriage rates, divorce rates, murder rates, or any other social problem. No intelligent argument could be made that Black people are better off because of the "discovery" of the Willie Lynch speech, so there is no practical value in promoting it.

11. The fake speech completely disregards the great tradition of African American resistance to enslavement. Herbert Aptheker in *American Negro Slave Revolts* (1965) documents numerous uprisings, and this is only one form of this tradition of resistance. There were other forms of African cultural resistance to social disintegration. For example, in *Slave Culture* (1987), Sterling Stuckey documents the retention of African culture through rituals such as the *ring shout,* which is a traditional sustained practice in the African community where men and women move in a circle in a counterclockwise direction, shuffling their feet, clapping, and often spontaneously singing or praying aloud. This ritual helped sustain African American communities and became central to the cultural transmission of African traditions into Black life in America.

However, many Willie Lynch promoters falsely believe that if it is pointed out that African social structure held the dominant influence on Black life even in the midst of slavery, then somehow it is being argued that slavery was not a brutal institution. They incorrectly believe that it is either one or the other, but it is actually both/and, meaning that slavery was a vicious institution *and* the traditional African social structure provided an effective defense against complete social disintegration. The Lynch supporters should be proud to come from such a strong heritage that was able to sustain itself through one of the greatest tragedies in human history rather than thinking that Euro-Americans are being "let off the hook" for slavery.

To assume that naïve Black people were simply controlled and manipulated by the all-wise slave owners would require a total dismissal of the evidence of plantation and city life during slavery. The fact must be acknowledged that African culture was resilient enough to sustain itself throughout several hundred years of the vicious slave system. In the words of the poet Maya Angelou, "Still I Rise."

12. The "speech" promotes ignorance of the negative impact of the 20th century on Black family and community life. For years the works of E. Franklin Frazier and Stanley Elkins had been accepted as the definitive history of Black families, and both writers concluded that slavery destroyed the Black family and decimated Black culture. However, this thesis about the Black family was first challenged by John Blassingame, author of *The Slave Community* (1972), whose use of slave narratives indicated that in the slave quarters, Black families existed as functioning institutions.

Other studies also challenged the Franklin-Elkins thesis, but it was the landmark study by Herbert Gutman, *The Black Family in Slavery and Freedom: 1750-1925* (1976), that put to rest the enduring myth that the Black family was destroyed during slavery. Through the use of plantation birth records and marriage applications, Gutman concluded that the two-parent household was the dominant family form during slavery. Using census data for a number of cities between 1880 and 1925, Gutman found that the majority of Black people of all social classes were living in nuclear families as opposed to single-parent homes. Their family forms evolved from family and kinship patterns that had originated from African extended family values and communal behavior patterns. As sociologist Robert Staples states, "[T]hese historical studies demonstrate that the Black family was a stable unit during slavery and in the immediate post-slavery years. The rise in out-of-wedlock births and female-headed households are concomitants of twentieth century urban ghettos" (Staples, *The Black Family,* 6th ed., pp. 4-5).

It was the triple negative factors of *migration*, *urbanization*, and *integration* during the "Jim Crow" era which brought about the disintegration of the Black community in the mid-20th century, and to ignore these potent factors is misguided. (See Part II for a detailed discussion). The divorce rate was never an issue in the Black community until the 1960s, and in fact it was California's Family Law Act of 1969 (went into effect on January 1, 1970) passed by Governor Ronald Reagan, which created the "no fault divorce" that has caused a great deterioration of the Black family. The vast majority of us born in the South can still remember that our grandparents and great grandparents were in married relationships and maintained two-parent households.

Further, there were no Black gangs, black-on-black violence, disrespect of elders, or abuse of women in the Black community until the 20th century. The triple negative factors of migration, urbanization, and integration have had a far more destructive impact on the social fabric of Black community life and marriage than slavery did, despite the savagery of the U.S. slave system. To dismiss the 20th century origin of these problems as unimportant would be foolish to say the least. Any solution-oriented person knows that to solve a social problem, one must first determine the true source of the problem rather than invent silly myths about its origin.

Appendix I

Conversation with and Confession Letter from the Alleged Forger of the "Willie Lynch Speech"

The following confession letter was written and emailed to me on November 30, 2009 by Dr. Kwabena Faheem Ashanti. However, I did not actually read his email and the attached confession letter until early February 2010. I receive so many emails regarding the Willie Lynch hoax that I do not always look at them with any urgency.

Around February 7, 2010, I had some downtime while caring for a family member in the hospital and decided to use my laptop and begin reading the backlog of old emails. When I came across Ashanti's email, I vaguely remember quickly scanning over it a couple months earlier, but there was nothing in the subject heading that caught my attention, so I moved on to others emails. This time, however, I was carefully reading each email to determine if I should reply, file it in a folder, or delete it. When I read Ashanti's confession letter, I was stunned that I missed it the first time.

This is the text of the email he sent to me:

> *This is your brother Dr. K.F. ASHANTI hear [sic] in Durham, NC. I am confiding in you to hold this in confidence until I have finished the third edition of my book. You can say, however, I know who has calmied [sic] to be the author without revealing it until I release you. You may even interview me by telephone. You, I do respect. This is my Mobil [sic] number…*

After reading Dr. Ashanti's email and confession letter, I thought that this could be an amazing development in exposing the origins of the Willie Lynch hoax, so I put together a list of twelve questions and made it a priority to call him the next day to see if his claim was credible. Not only was the telephone number valid, but everything that Ashanti told me about his professional background and current work in the conversation turned out to be true.

We had a cordial 90-minute conversation in which I asked him many tough questions, such as when and why he wrote the fake speech, why he chose the name "Willie Lynch," to whom did he initially distribute the speech, did anyone else help him write it, what sources did he use, and what made him come out and confess now.

In response to these questions, Ashanti stated that while he lived in Durham, North Carolina in the 1970s, he created various fake "documents" because there were no Black bookstores or other resources in the area that he could use for information or historical facts. Although he was a member of a local study group, Ashanti claims to have written the Lynch speech by himself in 1979 on an old-fashioned typewriter as a leaflet to secretly distribute and inform the local Black community.

He had already earned his Ph.D. and feared that he would be fired if his name was associated with the Lynch speech. He further stated that he made up the name "Willie" because it is a common name that people in the South could relate to, and he was thinking about Lynchburg, Virginia, when he came up with the name "Lynch." Ashanti did not remember why he chose the year "1712," and stated that after distributing the leaflet, he did not really think much about it again until many years later when people continued to reference this "document." As an experienced professional researcher, I analyzed all of his responses and they made sense, including his background as a Black psychologist specializing in brainwashing techniques.

After the conversation, I had enough information to further investigate his claims, and after our second interview (lasting an hour and 15 minutes) on February 15, I became satisfied that not only did all of his comments regarding his academic and professional background check out, he has more to lose in his professional career than he stands to gain by falsely claiming to be the author of arguably one of the greatest urban legends among Black folks in the Western hemisphere.

One purpose of the interview was for me to examine his motives, and thus of all the questions, the one that I was very curious about hearing his response to was why he decided to confess now. Ashanti indicated that he was casually searching the internet for some information, and he unexpectedly saw a link to my first Lynch essay and decided to look at it. In the essay, I clearly indicate that the forger was a young African American male in the 20s-30s age range, and that I was so precise in indicating the forger's background that he said, "Damn, the brother got me!"

He also stated that "you convinced me to come clean." In his email, Ashanti asked me not to reveal his name until after his next book is finished because he later stated that he would include a "confession chapter" in the book. The third edition of his book on brainwashing is now available, but I do not have a copy, and thus I am unaware if he included such as chapter.

We cannot be 100 percent certain that Dr. Kwabena Faheem Ashanti wrote the original version of the "Willie Lynch Speech" in 1979 as he alleges since he no longer has a copy, but after interviewing him twice and investigating his background, it is my professional opinion that the preponderance of the evidence clearly leans towards his claim being true.

—Professor Manu Ampim
Oakland, California

Publisher's Note: Since being exposed, Kwabena Ashanti has now indicated in recent 2013 radio interviews that he created the fake Willie Lynch speech in *1976*, instead of 1979 as he stated in his earlier "confession letter" sent to Professor Ampim in 2009.

Email and Confession Letter from Alleged Forger

Who Wrote the Lynch Speech? Email

It is **Prof. Manu Ampim** that gets the credit for discovering and revealing that the ***Willie Lynch Speech*** was and still is a FAKE !!!! Look at what he concluded about the "speech":

> *It is clear that the "Willie Lynch Speech" is a late 20th century invention because of the numerous reasons outlined in this essay.*
>
> *I would advance that the likely candidate for such a superficial speech is an African American male in the 20s-30s age range, who probably minored in Black Studies in college. He had a limited knowledge of 18th century America, but unfortunately he fooled many uncritical Black people.*
>
> *Some people argue that it doesn't matter if the speech is fact or fiction, because white people did use tactics to divide us. Of course tactics were used but what advocates of this argument don't understand is that African people will not solve our problems and address the real issues confronting us by adopting half-baked urban myths.*

The Confession Letter

Finally, **I Kwabena Faheem Ashanti, PhD,** do willfully – but reluctantly – confess that **I am the originator of the very first version of the Willie Lynch letter in 1979.** I had earned my PhD degree in 1974 from the University of Pittsburgh in the Department of Counseling Education in the discipline of **Counseling Psychology.** My focus was in **Black (African) Counseling.**

I return to teach at North Carolina Central University in the department of Psychology as an Associate Professor. Prior to that I had served as the Director of Freshman Counseling at Fayetteville State University from 1970 to 1973. Yes, I did earned my PhD in only one year.

In 1979 I was 35 years old. Moreover, I was self-taught in African and Black Studies. Yes, I did *have a limited knowledge of 18th century America, and unfortunately I did fool many uncritical African American people.*

Author's Note: *The above undated confession letter was sent as an attachment with an email on November 30, 2009. When he contacted me, the alleged forger indicated that he was not ready for me to release the letter because it would appear in the third edition of his book Psychology of Brainwashing. The actual title of Ashanti's book is Psychotechnology of Brainwashing.*

Appendix II

Email and Phone Responses

I have received hundreds of email and phone responses since I began writing about the Willie Lynch hoax in 2005. I rarely made notes of these phone conversations, but I received calls from people of all levels of society. The calls were primarily from the U.S., Britain, and the Caribbean.

A few of these calls stood out, such as a call I received from someone in Chicago who was a former campaign director for Rev. Jesse Jackson. She wanted to thank me for my work and to inform me that she had always advised Jackson never to mention this myth. Other callers simply wanted to say thank you and make sure that I was a real person. Then, there were others who called out of anger to release some frustration about my taking away their myth.

Fortunately, I have a record of most email responses. Below is a good sample of the many email messages that I continue to receive from various people. These emails fall into three groups: (1) People who always knew that the Willie Lynch Speech was a modern forgery, (2) those who originally believed the speech to be authentic until they read my work, and (3) the 10 percent of people who will never admit that their myth is not true.

Below you will find examples of email messages from the three groups. They have been organized into the three groups for clarity and edited to correct grammatical errors, but the original voice of the sender has been maintained.

First Group (People who always knew that it was fake)

Received: Wednesday, February 22, 2012
Subject: Willie Lynch Letter

Hello,

I would like to personally thank you for all the research, time, and effort you put into deciphering one of the greatest shadows cast over Black Americans. I actually never thought to challenge the authenticity of the letter. I thought it was real. I did however find it weird that it was so short, [lacked detail], and frankly gave no real "pointers" on how to tame anyone! Also, if it was a speech, how could anyone know it word-for-word if in 1712 there were no video or audio recordings?

There were definitely some moments of doubt, but I just brushed it off and kept it moving. I never shared the letter with people or really discussed it besides with one person in my entire life. What I will share is the fact that the letter is a big hoax. I believe it was a modern day attempt to get Black people to see life the way the writer of the letter sees it. You did a wonderful job breaking the letter down. I hope the real writer comes forward someday. If not, then this will be one of the greatest mysteries or debatable topics in history once the question of validity becomes just as mainstream as the letter itself. I thank you again for that information.

Received: Wednesday, January 18, 2012
Subject: Willie Lynch Fraud

Professor Ampim:

Just took a look at the third installment in the Willie Lynch fraud series. Right on, brother! I shared your information with my students in my African American History since 1865 class. Some gave me shocked looks when they heard there was no [such] person as Willie Lynch. Thanks for the work, brother. It was an excellent forensic analysis that needs to be read far and wide.

Received: Saturday, February 6, 2010
Subject: Willie Lynch Syndrome

Good Evening Professor,

I have just had the pleasure of reading your essays regarding the "Willie Lynch" speech supposedly given in 1712. I must admit that I was fairly naive to the notion and/or person until a co-worker brought it to my attention, citing that the "divide and conquer" speech was and is the reason for the social [woes] that Blacks suffer through today. Considering her frequent references to the "speech" and ideology, I decided to do a little research of my own to get a better understanding of the message and an idea of how I could combat or support the processing of the information. Much to my dismay, I noticed some of the very same things you mentioned while reading the "original speech."

It is so disheartening to have such misinformation perpetuated, knowing that there are real issues that Black people face on a daily basis. Although the speech and its steps appear to have a level of authenticity, I cannot get past the use of "current" terminology nor can I ignore the chronological errors.

As a professional and a student, I would like to know if you have any other works that are available as research material on this subject, or can you direct me to more [publications] on the issue. I would like to share this information with my co-worker, so she can be fully informed on the matter and so she can make a decision on whether she is going to continue to spread this information as a truth or if she is going to recant all of her ravings about this person who single handedly devised a plan to encourage the self destruction of a race of people to last 300 years or longer.

Received: Wednesday, December 9, 2009
Subject: Willie Lynch

This is a very interesting fact. I'm ashamed to say I've never heard of Willie Lynch until Denzel Washington mentioned him in the movie *The Great Debaters*. Willie Lynch was figured into the storyline of that movie. But if Willie Lynch is an urban legend....even Hollywood wants us to believe he existed....why would he be mentioned in a movie....if in fact Willie Lynch didn't exist?

You learn something new every day. Thanks for your insight.

Received: Wednesday, April 8, 2009
Subject: Lynch Letter Analysis

Dear Professor Manu:

Thank you for your analysis of the Lynch letter. I teach and research in African American studies and have always wondered about its popularity. Just last week my students asked me what I thought about the letter, and this question put me in touch with your short essay. The documentary analysis is very nicely done and one which I intend to work through with my students this week. Thanks again.

Received: Wednesday, December 10, 2008
Subject: Willie Lynch Hoax

Good afternoon,

I'm a student at Springfield College in Massachusetts, and I will be obtaining a BS in Science by the end of next year. I'm writing to you because I'm one of those affected by the Willie Lynch letter, and I will say positively affected because "usually" experiences in life teach individuals valuable lessons, but sarcasm aside, I believe this one is of relevant importance….

The issue is that during our second class the Willie Lynch letter was a topic of discussion. Our teacher presented this letter to the class, and I'm sure that you will know the reaction of the students in the class. I think [it] is important to mention that the majority of the alumni are African American, a few whites, and seldom Puerto Rican. I will say that each person was outraged [regardless of his or her] nationality, which is good. It demonstrates that people are more empathetic. Bottom line is that I was somewhat uneasy about this letter because we are reading a book from a great historian *(A People's History of the United States* by Howard Zinn), and there's not a single mention of this letter. Something was not falling into place.

At home with the time and patience, I decided to [do] research about this strange letter, and I found reputable information that questioned the authenticity about this letter. With proof in hand, I had a dilemma. [Do] I have to tell my professor? How do I go about it? See the problem is that our professor has some sort of a huge ego, and I have to admit that, I'm not all confident about myself, and I did not want a bad grade. I looked for another way of telling her without getting myself in a jam.

I made copies of your investigation (parts I & II), and I delivered them anonymously to her school mailbox. I have to say to her defense, that I'm on an accelerated program; therefore, we don't meet regularly, but I did deliver the packet (your stuff, plus some other) a month before our last class. Our last class was this past Saturday, and I was expecting some sort of reaction. I didn't care how she presented the information, but I was expecting [her to correct the misinformation] and to give us a lesson on verifying sources, to go beyond making sure that we are not just learning crap and to let students know that this was not accurate information. Well, big disappointment, she did not mention anything. I don't want to discredit her in front of class, she's a great teacher, and anyone can make a mistake. But I also fear that someone else will not be as considerate, and if she mentions it again, will make a fool of her.

I can say that I did my part, but if by any chance you have any suggestions, please pass them along. They will always be welcome. Thanks for your time and the time invested in presenting us with accurate information.

Received: Wednesday, December 10, 2008
Subject: Lynch Speech

Dear Professor:

I thank you for your research on the infamous Willie Lynch

story. As a history teacher in a diverse high school in Chicago, I cover closely and sensitively the issue of American slavery. Upon hearing of the letter, I became very critical of its truth and asked myself many questions. I'm glad that you have thoroughly rebuked the myth.

I also receive regular requests from a local pastor to discuss it with his African-American congregation. He continues to insist even after I have told him I question its accuracy and therefore would prefer not to. When he asks again, I will give him copies of your report.

Received: Monday, December 1, 2008
Subject: Happy to See Death of the Willie Lynch Speech

Prof. Ampim,

I was very happy to find your essay, dispelling the myth of Willie Lynch. I am a student at Virginia Commonwealth University, who is conducting her own research on the topic. I wanted to know what made you write this, and why do you think that other scholars do not address this issue? I find it infuriating to find Willie Lynch in books, movies, and magazines. Why isn't more being done to explain the truth?

Response:

Thank you for your positive feedback. The timing of your email is interesting because I just returned from Richmond and Jamestown only a week ago, and it was my first visit to the area.

I decided to write a response to the Willie Lynch (WL) myth

because three years ago I was asked to participate in a local Oakland, CA panel discussion concerning the African "Maafa" (disaster, holocaust, or great tragedy). I decided that if I was going to spend my time addressing this issue of the enslavement of African people and its aftermath, then I would make an important contribution to changing the way Black people think about our condition here in the U.S. After giving my slide presentation on the WL myth to an audience that was stunned, I then decided to publish my presentation to make my analysis available to a wider audience.

Scholars do not address the WL issue because it is a kindergarten myth that no credible historian would take seriously. Scholars tend to avoid dealing with internet myths and urban legends. On the other hand, I see the need to address some of these internet myths because the average person takes them seriously, and scholarship should always be made relevant to the needs of the community.

Advancing the work,
Manu Ampim

Received: Thursday, November 6, 2008
Subject: Willie Lynch Letter

Dr. Ampim,

My brother got a hold of the Willie Lynch speech and had been hounding me for the past month to read it. I never believed its authenticity, and now after reading it, it is as bad as I thought it would be, so I got online to research its origin and/or a critique of [it]. That's when I came across parts I and II of your Death of the Willie Lynch Speech, which was very enlightening. I agree with your critique.

Received: Monday, September 15, 2008
Subject: RE: Willie Lynch Challenge

Greetings, thank you for the information, and I will continue to search for the truth about the relevance of what [has caused] the breakdown [of] the black community. If you have any recommendations on readings, I would greatly appreciate it. I am very concerned about the African American community.

Response:

I am glad to receive your response. There are various sources, but I would recommend that maybe you can start with reading *The Black Family: Essays and Studies* (1999), edited by Robert Staples.

Also, if you look into the 1969 No-Fault Divorce Law, signed by then California Gov. Ronald Reagan, you will see how the divorce rate among Black people and all racial groups in America skyrocketed. After the California law, nearly all states around the country passed this same law making it very easy for married couples to divorce. This law changed the dynamics and damaged married life in America.

Another issue in terms of breaking up the black community is the introduction of crack-cocaine into our communities in the mid-1980s. The U.S. government sponsored this criminal activity, and you can read about it in the book by Gary Webb, *Dark Alliance: CIA, the Contras, and the Crack Cocaine Explosion* (2003).

Received: Sunday, December 30, 2007
Subject: Willie Speech

Hello Professor,

I live in Philadelphia and am of 33 years of age. I happened to run into your "Death of the Willie Lynch Speech" on the internet this evening. Curiosity struck when I was watching the film *The Great Debaters.* I am here writing to you to tell you how moving, eye-opening and well-written your speech was/is. I am one who dropped out of high school and decided to educate myself on various subjects. I was not aware of the history of the 1700s. If I had not run into your speech, I too may have been one of the few (or many) persons to believe in the Lynch speech. I thank you for writing and bringing light to the inaccuracy of the speech. I will share it with my colleagues and continue to search for further truths in controversial subjects.

Received: Friday, October 5, 2007
Subject: Willie Lynch

Professor Ampim:

Good afternoon. I read with interest your article "Death of the Willie Lynch Speech" (Part 1). For years I've been suspicious of the authenticity of this "speech." Like you I recognized words in the many versions of the "speech" that sounded way too 20th century for a letter/speech presumably from 1712.

The word "kits," as in "Gentleman these kits are your keys to control," always sounded out of place for a document claimed to be written in 1712. Other references sound out of place idiomatically.

More importantly, like you I just could not swallow this notion that white people have been able to control the minds and actions of Black people for 300 years based on some ideas set down by this man Willie Lynch. I too find the name suspicious.

What does it say about those of us who believe that the ghost of Willie Lynch and his "kits" are influencing the way we perceive and treat one another? It plays right into the hands of all those racists who feel Black people are unthinking and subhuman.

Furthermore, the so-called Willie Lynch Syndrome lets us off the hook in handling those issues that rightfully are our responsibility to handle (again, how we treat one another, etc.).

I am glad that you have poked substantial holes in this urban myth, but I know a lot of our people are holding on to it for dear life because they-and they'd deny the hell out of it-truly believe that white people have this awesome power over Black people.

Ironically, just yesterday on a local Black radio talk show here in Houston, old Willie Lynch was referenced as the reason why we are how we are!

I don't know when, or even if, we will be able to kill this Willie Lynch myth but someone needs to take it head on in a forum that reaches the majority of Black people. Because this persistent, and pernicious, belief in a magical "kit" that white people employ to control Black people is doing a great deal of harm to our people.

2nd Group (My Essay Changed Their Minds)

Received: Wednesday, March 3, 2010
Subject: Your Willie Lynch Speech Analysis

Dear Prof Ampim:

Thank you for your excellent scholarship exhibited in analysing the Willie Lynch speech. I must say that until I read your part I, I believed it because I wanted to and it suited my own purpose. If there is one [thing] I admire it is excellent scholarship and rigorous analysis, and your first piece made me think.

Received: Saturday, February 13, 2010
Subject: Willie Lynch hoax

Thank you so much for your research, brother. I first heard about the letter in college and believed it to be authentic. This was so easy to do because of the very obvious divisions we face amongst our people today, as outlined in the letter. I felt myself to be of a certain group that understood why us black folk are "divided." I heard Dick Gregory say something about it being a hoax last night and read your essay.

I am blown away to know that it is a hoax, and now I'm at a loss for trying to understand our issues. I am now interested in reading about Frederick Douglass to further my understanding of where we come from, though I know this will only scratch the surface. I am a spoken word artist, and have access to radio stations that can potentially reach millions. This will more than likely be the inspiration of my next piece.

Received: Wednesday, July 29, 2009
Subject: Death of the Willie Lynch Speech

Prof. Manu Ampim,

I just read your article, and I must say that it was very enlightening. I have considered the Willie Lynch Letter to be authentic ever since my father gave it to me to read about four years ago, until now. Unfortunately, as I began reading your article, I became upset that you would discount such a powerful letter until reading Part II, specifically "Negative Effects of the 20th Century."

As soon as possible, I plan to share your article with my parents, both well-educated African Americans, who also assumed (I think) the Willie Lynch Speech to be true.

Received: Tuesday, March 17, 2009
Subject: Willie Lynch?????

Greetings Professor Manu,

I recently read The Willie Lynch letter for the first time. Reading this document was a bittersweet experience for me. It was bitter because of the visual proof of most of the issues listed within the document as soon as I walk out of my bedroom door. The sweet part is that it urged me to research documents supporting Willie Lynch. The first document I came across happened to be "Death of The Willie Lynch Speech" written by you. As you elaborated on why the speech is bogus, my eyes opened up wider than ever before as I intend to research each person with first-hand accounts of slavery and slave owners tactics that you listed.

I have a 10 year-old son that I want to raise with a better awareness of our history in this country as well as the history that we were disconnected from. I appreciate your writing because I was ready to take Willie Lynch and run with it. Thank you for pointing out the error in doing so.

Received: Sunday, March 01, 2009
Subject: Thank you, sir.

Hello Professor. I am a soldier in the U.S. Army and deeply into Black history. I would have never figured out that the Willie Lynch letter was fake had I not read your essay. Even after reading W.E.B. DuBois, Fredrick Douglass, and various other authors of the sort, I was extremely quick to accept the letter as true. As you have stated, I shared the letter with some of my friends and family, and I am currently going back to add a note that it is unauthentic.

Received: Tuesday, June 03, 2008
Subject: Willie Lynch

Prof. Ampim,

I would like to add my thanks to the chorus of the second of the three groups noted in "Death of Willie Lynch Speech, Part II." I have prided myself on being quick to always look for evidence to support or dispute the many claims sent to me by email. In this case, I was given the book *The Willie Lynch Letter and the Making of a Slave,* and because of the subject matter and the reputation of the individual from whom I was receiving it, I quickly hurried to Amazon.com to find my own copy. I even encouraged my colleague's plan to purchase the book and have everyone he gave it to place their name in the book and pass it on to someone else to help "get the word out."

I have since sent Parts I and II of your essay to anyone to who I even casually mentioned the book. I hope your work will become something of an interfuron that will help us to become more resistant to the virus of the Willie Lynch Speech and embolden our social immune system against such works of distraction.

Received: Tuesday, April 08, 2008
Subject: Willie Lynch

Professor Manu Ampim,

I had disgraced myself. I considered myself, and I am considered by many, to be a serious student of history, but I was extremely perturbed with myself to discover that this "Willie Lynch Letter" is nothing more than a clever hoax. I am in debt to you for your essays, "Death of the Willie Lynch Speech." This simply tells me that I must to improve my critical thinking and analysis skills and that I am not as grounded in my subject matter as I once thought. If I am to be taken seriously as a creditable and reliable historian, I must not be so gullible and must developed advanced critical thinking skills. One day I hope to be counted among the stars of great black historians such as you, but it truly is a work in progress. Thank you for your truly vital and enlightening essays. You have allowed me to save face by not repeating that nonsense to anyone else.

Received: Tuesday, January 8, 2008
Subject: Willie Lynch Letter

Prof. Manu:

Thank you for the research. I'm in the number of those who took the letter as coming from history, and as a truth. Your research does make one realize the need for critical thinking to come forth in our thought processing. Forgive me, but I'm guilty of not utilizing critical thinking. Thank you for doing just that.

My first reading of the Willie Lynch letter was in the early 70s. It was brought to my attention while learning at a research center in the neighborhood. The research center was about teaching Black youths and adults to research things through reading. The center was constantly showing/demonstrating to us that everything we wanted, or had a need to know, was in a book/manual or some literature form.

I recalled it was so real to me (the Willie Lynch Letter which was taken from a book) that I retyped it, paid for copies, and gave out as many copies as I could. I was in my late twenties then. Sometime in the late eighties or early nineties, the Willie Lynch letter surfaced in the workplace. It became a topic of interest. Again I made copies and had no problem passing them out to all that took one. I place[d] the letter in seats, on tables, anywhere I could. That is just how much I wanted our people to know about how we had been (I thought/believed) set up. I gave very little thought that the letter may not be true. However, in the early nineties or late eighties, when the letter had surfaced in the workplace, I had experienced on my own by then, how trickery (divisiveness) was being played out in the workplace by the plantation overseers (i.e., supervisors, house negroes, and subservient whites). Thus, my critical thinking may have opened a little, not enough however, to dismiss the letter as being a complete hoax, but (critically thinking) to use the letter for us as Black folks to understand that we must take care in never forgetting that there is always an enemy plotting, (certainly not for our good) and just because someone looks like you, do not dismiss the fact that they may be the enemy.

Received: Saturday, November 10, 2007
Subject: Willie Lynch

When I first heard about the Willie Lynch speech was during the Million Man March (1995). It sounded so real when Min. Louis Farrakhan mentioned it that I had to rush to find out more. I even used it when the Henrietta Slave exhibit came to Charlotte, NC, and I was a docent (1996). The crowd loved it. In my heart, I thought it was [a] fake because I had never read about it before. I have read the works of Lerone Bennett Jr., John Hope Franklin, and many other scholars, but I never heard any mention of The Willie Lynch letter. Yes, I must say the letter is very interesting, and it can get the attention of African-Americans. You mentioned that years from now people will forget about the Willie Lynch letter. I don't think they will forget even though it is [a] fake. It makes a great conversation.

Response:

You wrote: "In my heart, I thought it was [a] fake." Yet you still promoted the phony "WL speech" anyway. Unfortunately, you must not be aware, or even care, that there are many African Americans across the country who now have little or no respect for people who have deliberately misled them on this WL issue. You consciously betray the trust of Black people in the same way as the historical enemies of Black people. What else are you willing to be dishonest about?

You justify misinformation and falsehood because people "loved" the fake speech. The phony speech promotes a make-believe white man as a demi-god, and at the same time, it leaves Black people with nothing to do other than worship the influence of an omnipotent white guy 300 years after he allegedly lived.

The work of Frederick Douglass makes for a much more insightful and relevant discussion than the fake speech. Also, Douglass was one of the greatest political activists of the 19th century. His life's work is a more important example for Black people to follow than to sit around in awe of a mystical white man. Lastly, you should know that all silly myths rise and fall, and this one is no different.

Advancing the work,
Manu Ampim

Response:

You are right. Now I am enlightening our people about the myth!

Received: Tuesday, August 14, 2007
Subject: "Death of Willie Lynch"

Greetings Professor,

I am writing to personally thank you for your wonderful research and study of the "so-called" Willie Lynch Speech. I truly appreciate your effort and respect your approach to the entire idiocy. I am one who took for granted the authenticity of the document and proceedings. However, now that you have exposed these many voids of truth in the matter, I am prepared to march forward with your findings.

3rd Group (Still Believes the Myth)

Received: Thursday, May 19, 2011
Subject: Willie Lynch Speech

First off, I would like to say I enjoyed reading your article. It was informative. However, your response to those who didn't whole heartedly agree with your take on the "letters" actually reminded me of the letters themselves. I personally fell into all three of your categories: 1) I was suspect about the book [sic] because of the numerous grammatical errors and lack of substantiated sources. 2) While I have recommended that book to many people, I simply didn't have evidence to discredit the book although I found the core message of the book to be true. 3) This same argument can be applied to the "existence of God" debate. Although there are many unanswerable questions about God, and the fact is that the Bible itself can be scrutinized. At the end of the day, it all boils down to faith.

In my opinion, the Willie Lynch Letters are very important because the book itself is a double edged sword that needs to be dulled on one side. While the author's overall message is well meaning, I know many people who have taken the knowledge from that book and used the same strategies to turn women out. I have seen it with my own eyes. A guy goes to prison, reads that book, and comes out with a new outlook on life, but when reality hits him (He's a felon with no viable job skills or work history.) He implores the Willie Lynch tactics to recruit young women into prostitution. That book should be re-titled, The Perfect Blue Print for Manipulation.

I will copy and forward your essay to many others, but I will still recommend that book. If for no other reason than to keep people aware of ideals the book is trying to convey as well as how those same tactics are used to promote negativity. Again, I enjoyed reading your essay, and I don't discredit you in any way... but lighten up... it's like telling a "kid" there's no Santa, or Easter Bunny, or God. (Look as deep into that as you want.) The overall concept of those entities serves a greater justice, especially when it comes to God, Allah, Jah, Jehova, etc. Is something which represents pure love and goodness for man really manipulative or egocentric? As described in the Bible? (If you don't do this, something will happen to you. Obey me at all cost or that's your ass!) When used for the greater good, this stuff (along with the Willie Lynch Letters) serves a great purpose.

Received: Tuesday, October 27, 2009
Subject: Willie Lynch Letter

I just wanted to say that maybe it was never mentioned by former slave masters or slave owners in that era or by antislavery activists of that time for one reason. The slave masters or slave owners did not want others to find out about the "new plan of action" in case it was heard by the wrong ears, which also kept the antislavery activists from finding out in order to make any mention of the plan. Therefore, this is a reason as to why it had not been known.

Received: Saturday, October 03, 2009
Subject: Willie Lynch Speech

I think you are a white guy or an African from Africa whose ancestors helped put my ancestors on the boat. However, I could be wrong. Someone needs to look you up and find out who you are. Obviously you have never heard your grand-mother or great grandmother tell the stories of the past (slavery days).

Received: Friday, January 23, 2009
Subject: Willie Lynch

Dear Professor Ampim,

I am a white U.S. History teacher who teaches at Brookwood High School in Gwinnett County, GA. While studying slavery, I have read your response to my classes composed of African-Americans, whites and other races. I have never seen a more profound reaction to anything I have ever taught. Eyes were truly opened as never before. But as you said, there are 10 per-cent out there that won't accept it.

In fact complaints have been filed against me by some of the African American students. I am facing disciplinary action for this and other comments I make about race trying to dispel some of the myths, untruths, misconceptions, stereotypes, etc. that we educators must overcome in order to really teach all of our kids the truth about our history. I do not sugar-coat anything whether it makes whites look badly, Blacks look badly, or any other group. I am on a lifelong quest for the truth because I want to inspire my students to be better citizens.

Received: Friday, January 25, 2008
Subject: On the Willie Lynch Letter.

Professor Ampim, I was curious if you had read this book, and if you had changed your opinion or if this book was suspect: *Willie Lynch, Real or Imaginary.*

Response:

Thank you for your inquiry. The author of this book emailed probably around early last year to inform me that his book had been published.

Unfortunately, the book is amateurish and misleading propaganda to say to the least. The author's work is so superficial that he does not know how to spell Frederick Douglass' last name, and it never occurred to him that the Douglass Papers are in the Library of Congress in Washington, DC, and there is not one document authored by Douglass regarding some alleged Willie Lynch "handbook." William Lynch is a common English name, but the author failed to establish a William Lynch in Virginia giving a speech in 1712. Nor can he account for where the fake speech came from in the 1990s. The goal of the book is political propaganda and not scholarship.

Advancing the work,
Manu Ampim

Received: Saturday, January 12, 2008
Subject: My Opinion

Dear Sir/Madam,
I have just read correspondence about the Willie Lynch Letter being a myth. I don't believe it's a myth because first of all, everything that it says shows that its truth by the way Black people are today. They did try all those tactics and other tactics that we may not know about against us because you can see it in Black people today. They have set out to destroy us as a race so that we can always serve them forever, and there is no better way to do that than to make us inferior to them. They treated us like their property and like we were their pets and tried to destroy our intelligence and making us 3/5th of a man. Those particular tactics are affecting us today, and before the Willie Lynch Letter came out, we had no idea why we acted the way we acted and why we relate to one another the way we do and how we view white people.

We have always wondered why we couldn't trust one another, unite with one another, and love, care, or share with one another like humans. We wondered why we always felt inferior to white people and light-skinned people, why we couldn't run or support our own businesses, why we couldn't follow and trust in our leaders, why we sell each other out, why we desire to integrate with white people and believe that without them we can't live or do for ourselves. If the Willie Lynch method was not true, then tell us what method they really used back during the time of slavery and after slavery. Now if you are going to take that away and say that wasn't true now we need to know the absolute truth, and we as a people need to know that right now.

Received: Thursday, September 27, 2007
Subject: Willie Lynch

Does it matter if the speech is authentic? Does it matter if there was a man named Willie Lynch? For me, it doesn't. If the speech inspires determination to free oneself from the psychological bondage--More Power to it!

Call him Willie Smith for all I care. Is the letter accurate in its depiction of the inhumane treatment and trauma inflicted on the Black American? It most certainly is!

Response:

You are free to continue believing in silly fairy tales and urban mythology. Unfortunately, you are sadly mistaken in your assertion that the fake speech is helping Black people free themselves from psychological bondage. In fact, the opposite is true. The worshippers of "Willie Lynch" have given this mythical white man insurmountable god-like powers, that he can give one speech and magically control 40 million Black people in America 300 years later. The mental enslavement in worshipping an omnipotent Willie Lynch is obvious. It is a shame that adults in our community know almost nothing about our experience in America, and rather than find the origins of our problems in order to bring about solutions, they would rather sit around believing in kindergarten myths.

Anyone who is genuinely working on solving our problems is *always* concerned about how these problems developed. **My sister, you apparently don't understand that the origin and the solution to a problem are intimately linked. No intelli-**

gent person can separate the two unless he or she has no interest in a solution.

If you are serious, then read about how our current problems developed largely in the 20th century with migrations, urbanization, and integration (See Part II).

Advancing the work,
Manu Ampim

About the Author

Professor Manu Ampim is an historian and primary (first-hand) researcher specializing in Africana Studies.

He has taught in the Department of History at Morgan State University (Baltimore, MD) and at San Francisco State University in the Department of Ethnic Studies. Also, Ampim has studied at Oxford University in England and collaborated on a NASA-sponsored research project, which examined the ancient climate and migration patterns in Africa. Currently, Prof. Ampim teaches history at Contra Costa College (San Pablo, CA) and Africana Studies/Study Abroad at Merritt College (Oakland, CA). He is also the Director of *Advancing the Research* in Oakland, CA.

Professor Ampim has lead numerous educational tours to Africa and Central America, and he has conducted extensive primary research at all of the major museums, institutes and libraries throughout America, Europe and Canada, which house ancient Egyptian, Nubian, and Kushite artifacts. Since the 1990s, he has conducted various field research projects in Egypt, Nubia, Sudan, and Ethiopia to continue his primary research at dozens of field sites.

Prof. Ampim has written pioneering books and essays on Black community development and other topics in Africana Studies. He has also written several essays in *Egypt: Child of Africa* (1994), edited by Ivan Van Sertima, and his most influential work will be his long-awaited book, *Modern Fraud* (2014), which is the documentation of the Rahotep and Nofret statues as among the greatest forgeries in the history of ancient African archaeology.

Prof. Ampim can be reached at:

P.O. Box 18623, Oakland, CA 94619 (USA)
Phone: 510-568-3880
Email: Profmanu@acninc.net
Website: www.ManuAmpim.com
www.SaveNubia.org

BCP Pamphlet Series

A Chronology of the Bible: Challenge to the Standard Version. Yosef ben-Jochannan. 1972*, 1995. 24 pp. $4.00. Dr. Ben traces some of the significant influences, developments, and people that have shaped and provided the foundation for the holy books used in the major western religions.

Africa the Wonder and the Glory. Anna Melissa Graves. 1942*, 1980. 43 pp. illus. $4.00. Graves uses this pamphlet to argue the priority of and the far reaching influence of African civilization.

Children of the Sun. George Wells Parker. 1918*, 1978. 31 pp. $4.00. Parker skillfully uses classical and contemporary sources to examine the African origins and influence throughout the African continent, the Arab world, Asia, and Europe.

The Tragedy of White Injustice. Marcus Garvey. 1935*, 1978. 24 pp. $4.00. In this epic poem, Garvey describes the legacy of White racism and colonialism.

Ethiopia and the Origin of Civilization. John G. Jackson. 1939*, 1985. 32 pp. $4.00. In this essay, Jackson discusses the ancient Ethiopians and their widespread influence on the early history of civilization.

The Negro's Contribution to Art. Charles Seifert. 1938,* 1980. 36 pp. illus. bibl. $4.00. Seifert argues that Africans were among the world's first artists.

Burning at Stake in the United States. The N.A.A.C.P. 1919*, 1986. 20 pp. $ 4.00. These accounts of five brutal human burnings that occurred during the summer of 1919 compel readers to establish an emotional link with America's horrific past.

The Ku Klux Spirit. J. A. Rogers. 1923*, 1980. 36 pp. $4.00. Rogers offers valuable insight into the history and origin of the Ku Klux Klan.

**Indicates first year published*

140922-300-12-60W

Peter Halldorf

To Love Your Neighbour's Church as Your Own

A manifest for Christian unity

To Love Your Neighbour's Church as Your Own

COVER DESIGN
Jonatan Palm
GRAPHIC DESIGN
Tellwell Talent
PRINTED WITH CONTRIBUTIONS FROM
Holy Covenant Evangelical Orthodox Church
www.holycovenanteoc.com
PRINT
Tellwell Talent

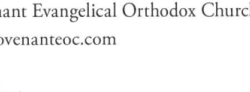

Tellwell Talent
www.tellwell.ca

ISBN
978-0-2288-0855-8 (Paperback)
978-0-2288-0856-5 (eBook)

Table of Contents

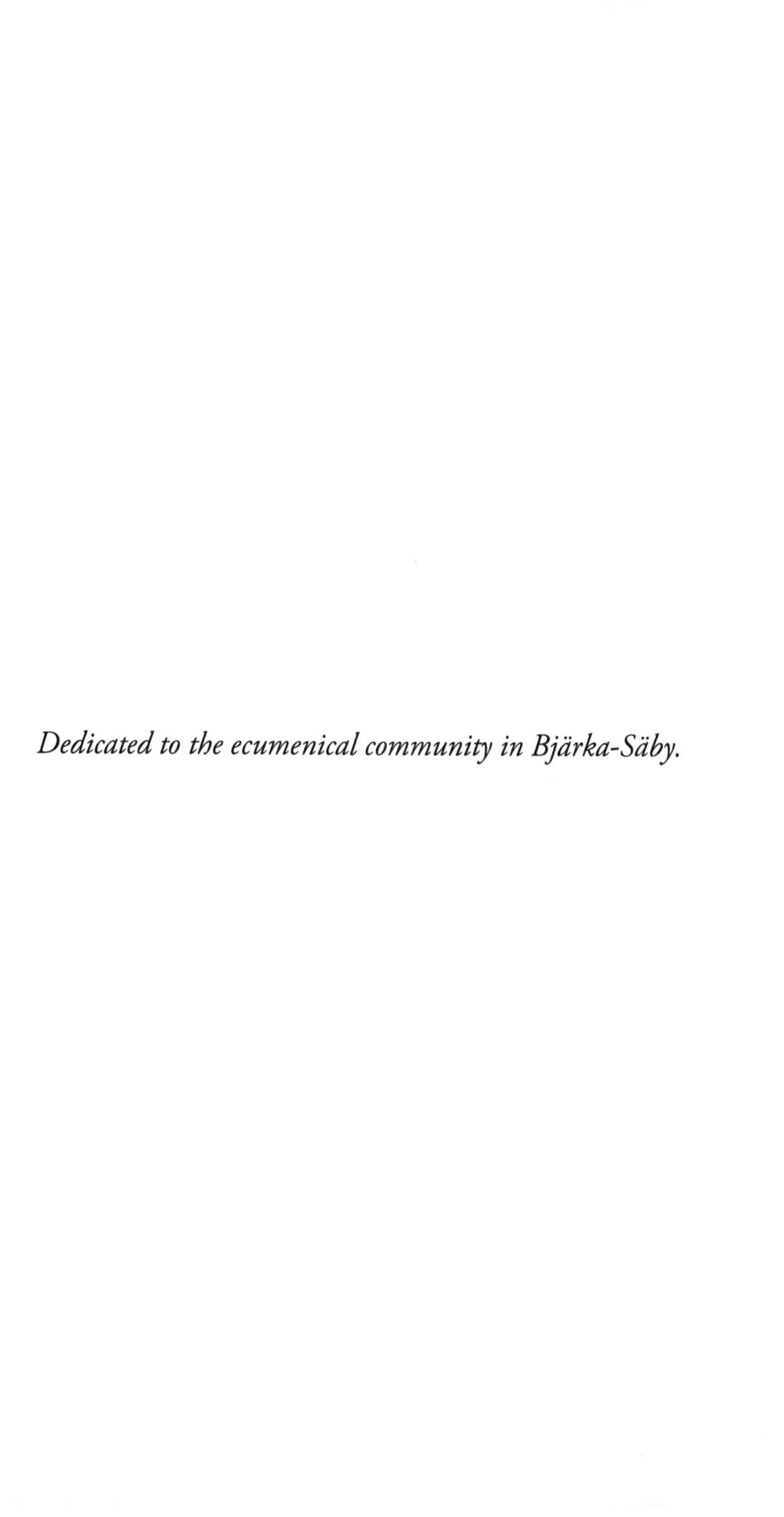

Dedicated to the ecumenical community in Bjärka-Säby.

Foreword

The Orthodox metropolitan Johannes Zizioulas described how ecumenism has three dimensions. He calls them the ecumenism in time, the ecumenism in space and existential ecumenism.

Within the ecumenism in time, we find the work of being reconciled as Christians based on our common 2,000-year-old history, the Bible and the Church fathers. This is the ecumenism that dominates the official ecumenical dialogues, and we are all aware this work is progressing at a very slow pace.

The ecumenism in space occurs when Christians from different parts of the world and different traditions come together to share their experiences, to pray together and to join in cooperative action and events. We give testimony to the catholicity of the Church every time this takes place.

These two vantage points have dominated the ecumenical landscape for the last couple of decades but Zizioulas would like to add a third dimension that he chooses to call existential ecumenism. He defines it as our cooperative desire to confront the crucial existential chal-

lenges that humanity is facing today – not only in certain places or certain circumstances. Ecology is one such area where Christians are challenged to stand together to address some of the dire situations impacting the world.

Zizioulas writes: "I see in it an important ecumenical dimension in that it brings the divided Christians before a common task which they must face together. We live at a time when fundamental existential problems overwhelm our traditional divisions and relativize them almost to the point of extinction. Look, for example, at what is happening today in the Middle East: do those who persecute the Christians ask them to which Church or Confession they belong? Christian unity in such cases is de facto realized by persecution and blood – an ecumenism of martyrdom."

This essay is my attempt to put into words what a contemporary ecumenical posture could look like, with this existential and spiritual perspective towards ecumenism at the forefront and through the lens of my ecclesial circumstance – the Pentecostal movement. This does not mean we can neglect the theological questions that still stand in the way of Christian unity. But, there are existential questions that need to take precedence. Unity, the issue that Jesus Himself prioritized: so that the world will believe. For this reason, a couple of words from the contemporary monastic father, Matta al-Miskin has become a point of reference to me: "We must start by living together in the one and innermost being of faith before we can agree on the content." Where do we begin? This is the question.

This essay has two parts. In the first part, which I've chosen to call *Manifest for Christian Unity*, the personal testimony takes front stage. People and communities that not only speak about, but also incarnate, unity in a radical vision of oneness keep the flame of hope alive. However,

there are stumbling blocks that we must acknowledge and confront. One of those is outlined in the second part of the book: *An Ecumenical Perspective Concerning the Office of Peter*. Here, as well as in many other situations, the reference point must be a Bible study. In the reflections about the pope, the bishop of Rome, I make reference to the ecumenically-minded orthodox theologian Olivier Clément and his book *You are Peter,* where he formulates a posture that we could potentially gather around.

Peter Halldorf
San Masseo, Assisi

I. Manifest for Christian Unity

1

During the 20th century a host of ecumenical movements were birthed and, independently of one another, put the question about the visible unity of the Church on the map. Already at the turn of that century, Elena Guerra, founder of the Order of the Oblates of the Holy Spirit, wrote 12 exhorting letters to Pope Leo XIII about renewed teaching concerning the Holy Spirit. She asked the pope to invite the faithful to rediscover a life in the Spirit and to encourage prayer for Christian unity.

In the following years, Pope Leo XIII distributed several important documents concerning the Holy Spirit and invited the Church to pray that the 20th century would become the century of the Holy Spirit. He introduced the so-called Pentecostal Novena, a nine-day time of prayer for spiritual renewal, between Ascension and Pentecost every year.

2

An answer to those prayers of the pope arrived six years later. On Azusa Street, a Los Angeles backstreet, behind a timber yard and some stables, the modern Pentecostal movement was born in April 1906. Within this movement, the gift of tongues caught some attention, but the most revolutionizing feature even offensive to some – was the way this movement broke down barriers between races, classes and churches.

William Seymour, the Afro-American front-figure of the moment wrote in 1906 about the fruits of the revival: "People came together ... became one, one bread, one

body in Jesus Christ. No Jew or heathen, slave or free in Azusa Street mission." In a society that was deeply segregated, Azusa Street revealed a revived humanity of reconciliation and unity between people. This was the greater miracle. The gift of tongues was just the confirmation that the language curse of Babel had been abolished. A new season had sprung with a communion that was not based on the colour of your skin.

3

William Seymour's vision of a church that proclaimed a new humanity with reconciliation among people was soon met with resistance. Within a couple of years, the ministry was split primarily because of white leaders in the movement who were scandalized by black people who were not "kept in their place."

Relentlessly Seymour encouraged people to love each other across the borders and challenged the privileged white class and the deeply rooted rules of segregation. He was defamed and accosted without responding in kind. Seymour combined integrity and charisma in a way that had a deep impact on his surroundings.

One contemporary of Seymour testifies: "This man indeed lived the very things we have been preaching for years. It was the outstanding character in this God-appointed man that drew people to these simple meetings."

Seymour became increasingly isolated because he refused to relinquish his radical vision for unity. He longed for a whole Church:

"O, my heart cries out to God that He would make every child of His see the necessity of living in the 17th

chapter of John, that we may be one body in Christ as Jesus has prayed," he said.

But, the time had not yet come for such a brave vision. When Seymour died in 1922 at the age of 52, he was almost totally forgotten. The medical reason for his death was a heart attack, but perhaps he died from a broken heart.

4

In 1923, a year after Seymour's death, Paul Couturier, a school teacher and priest in Lyon, France, began to use a lot of his spare time to aid thousands of Russians who had arrived in the city fleeing the Bolsheviks. It was his first encounter with a Christianity that was not Roman Catholic. From the Orthodox Christians that he helped he not only encountered new friendships but also other gifts. His heart awakened to the beauty of the liturgy of these people and the abandon of their faith.

Couturier became convinced of the necessity of Christian unity in the years that followed. In 1935, he was given the responsibility for the Octave for unity[1], with eight days of prayer that began within the Roman Catholic Church in 1908. He developed it into an international week of prayer for Christian unity. He chose a saying from the Metropolitan Gorodetsky of Kiev as the motto for the week: "The walls of separation do not rise as far as heaven."

---

1 The Week of Prayer for Christian Unity began in 1908 as the Octave of Christian Unity, and focused on prayer for church unity. It is still observed and celebrated every year between January 18th - 25th. www.oikoumene.org/en/press-centre/events/week-of-prayer-for-christian-unity

5

That same year - 1935 - Maria Gabriella Sagheddu travelled from Sardinia to the Trappist monastery Grottaferrata near Rome. She was born in 1915 and grew up in a poor shepherd's family on the Italian island. Maria was a gifted child but had to relinquish her high school education to care for her siblings and widowed mother.

In her earlier years, Maria did not appear to have any great interest in spiritual matters. However, at the age of 18, she experienced a radical conversion of the heart and was drawn into an intense life of prayer. She could often be found on her knees in the church praying before the sacrament.

Soon enough, Maria discerned that she wanted to enter a monastery and devote her whole life to God. At age 21, she left Sardinia and entered the monastery Grottaferrata, where she became known as Maria Gabriella. It was here that she encountered the ecumenism led by French priest Paul Couturier. After a liturgy in the monastery specifically focusing on the unity of the church, Maria experienced how the Lord spoke to her about living a life dedicated to the cause of Christian unity.

On that same night, Maria felt a sharp pain in her shoulder. Her physical health declined rapidly, and within a few months, Maria was diagnosed with tuberculosis. Her remaining time was spent praying the same prayer that Jesus Himself prayed to His Father: that the ones who believe in Him may be one.

The testimony of Maria Gabriella in many ways resembles other witnesses with a strong emphasis on ecumenism, but hers came to be received as a special sign because of her humility and simplicity. In the life of Maria

Gabriella, many Christians encountered a role model for how they could journey together toward deeper unity.

When the ecumenical movement within the Roman Catholic Church grew stronger, the life of Maria Gabriella became a source of inspiration. The way she offered herself as a sacrifice for the unity of the church deeply impacted people from many different traditions and countries.

Sister Maria Gabriella Sagheddu died April 23, 1939, at the young age of 25. She was canonized by Pope John Paul II in 1983 during the conclusion of the annual week of prayer for Christian unity, and since then her day of remembrance is celebrated on April 22. Maria Gabriella gave up her life to prepare the way for Christian unity through prayer.

6

Four years after Maria Gabriella's passing, on December 7, 1943, Chiara Lubich, a young Italian girl sealed her covenant with God. She did not suspect that this would be the beginning of a worldwide movement with millions of followers. The subsequent Focolare movement's two most distinguishing traits would become the work toward visible unity of the Church and the recognition of the abandoned Christ in humankind's abandonment of God.

For a long time, Lubich had sensed God was calling her to something particular. One day she crossed a railway and heard the voice of Christ, "Give your whole life to Me." Without a moment's hesitation, she contacted a priest and asked to devote her life to God.

Young women began to gather around Chiara Lubich. During the second world war bombings in Trento, they took refuge in different bomb shelters throughout the

town. In the glowing light of wax candles underground they read the Gospels and longed to openly practice the message contained therein. One day, in a dark basement, the young women randomly opened the Bible and landed in John 17: 21 "Father, that they may all be one." From that moment they knew they had been born into the world because of the words written on this page in the Bible. Their shared motto became: "Unity or death."

A couple of months earlier a priest had asked Chiara Lubich: "Do you know when Jesus experienced the most suffering?" To which she answered, "In the garden of Gethsemane." But the priest replied, "No. Jesus experienced the most suffering when He on the cross exclaimed, 'My God, my God, why have You forsaken Me?'

Those words struck Lubich and became foundational to the spirituality of Focolare: to recognize and to serve the abandoned and forsaken Christ in every person.

7

With young Chiara Lubich as leader, a movement recognized for its sacrificial service to the most vulnerable took shape. The few garments of clothing that they had were gathered in a pile, a way to share poverty and circumstance of the people. Books were stowed away in the attic for the purpose of gaining knowledge in a different way. The word "evangelization" was not used because of its sometimes politicized meaning. And, they began to see the love of God transforming the hearts of the people in new and unexpected ways.

Soon, there were 500 people in the small town of Trento, but it wouldn't be long before the movement spread

outside of Italy. In time, the Focolare movement spread worldwide, leaving a deep imprint, calling the Church back to the simple and radical message of the gospel.

During her lifetime, Chiara Lubich was recognized by four popes. She had opportunity to speak with religious and political leaders from around the world, including Orthodox patriarch Bartholomeus, who had visited her just a short time before her passing on March 14, 2008. Today, Focolare communities consist of both families and celibates in 182 countries.

8

Unity is the "first duty" within the Focolare movement. "May everything except unity fade away. Jesus is present where unity is present," writes Chiara Lubich. Few, if anyone, have in our time spoken so boldly about the unity of the Church as the most significant condition of faith. The way she and the Focolare movement encourages is the way of the cross, the way of self-emptying. By treating others wounds as they were our own – "to be the other," as Lubich expressed it, we follow the way of Jesus.

She speaks about how those in the young Focolare movement would train themselves in "becoming one" with others. "We have to empty our heads of ideas, our hearts of feelings and willpower, in order to be able to identify ourselves with the other," she said.

A particular joy is found on that road. The main task of the Focolare movement, according to its founders, was to present the world with joy. "Others are called to distribute bread, provide shelter, counsel or education," Lubich said. "Our vocation is to spread joy."

Joy sets the tone for the radical message of Christian discipleship, where we are exhorted to "embrace the forsaken Christ." The full paradox of the gospel takes shape here: the light countenance and the joy of the ones who have taken the sacrificial message of the gospel seriously. Through the life of Chiara Lubich, we glean the depths of the mystery of love. The contours of a life lived in and with Christ appear with rare clarity.

9

The word ecumenism, from the Greek word, *oikoumenikos*, literally means "that which concerns the inhabited world," that is to say *worldwide*. The immediate sign of the presence of the Holy Spirit on the day of Pentecost was the many tongues that were spoken, a confirmation that the Church from Her inception was ecumenical. Her horizon touches the whole inhabited world, all of humanity. She speaks all languages.

Contrary to the cult that exists for the few elect and testifies to the salvation of these few and the damnation of the others, the Church is present for the sake of the whole world. She has restored humanity in a microcosm. The good message of the gospel is presented to all people – everyone that has lived, everyone that is alive and everyone that will come into existence.

It is striking how spiritual renewal within the Church seems to go hand in hand with ecumenical movements. These spiritual renewals have vitalized how the vocation of every Christian is ecumenical in the deepest meaning of that word. At a time when sharp borders are drawn, when many people want to identify themselves with the

help of labels, once more we are challenged towards a new ecumenism. As Christians, we must always investigate our motivation toward this vocation.

Every group – every church, congregation and community – is tempted toward self-satisfaction, prejudice, exclusivity and the belief that we are the elected ones. One cannot simply become ecumenical by calling oneself ecumenical. One does not become ecumenical by presenting a smorgasbord of dishes from the worldwide Church to pick and choose from.

One becomes ecumenical primarily by loving those that are found outside of one's own circumstance. It was this love that was found in the heart of William Seymour on Azusa Street, that took hold of Paul Couturier in the encounter with the exiled Christians from Russia, that filled Sister Maria Gabriella's heart when the Lord spoke to her and that became Chiara Lubich's great joy in life. They became witnesses of the impossibility of a divided Christ. They are the forerunners who have brought us to where we are today.

10

"For he who is not against us is on our side."[2] The disarming, piercing words of Jesus make most Christians feel somewhat of a duty to pray for the unity of the Church. But, when engaging the question of unity, we are confronted with a mountain of obstacles. The various interpretations of the message Jesus proclaimed give further fuel to the fire of polemics between churches and Christians.

2 Mark 9:40

Gunnel Vallquist (1918 - 2016), one of the most relentless voices for Christian unity in Sweden in the last half-century, suggested there are two ways to face all the issues that provide fodder to the dissension between churches. The first and most difficult way is to tackle the points of division, one by one, in the hope that a greater common understanding is ultimately reached. This is the current method employed by the official work of ecumenism. It is a never-ending work and will probably not reach its aim before the end of time.

The second way, Vallquist suggests, is to approach the problem with a Gospel lens, through the words of Jesus Christ Himself. Like when He says, "If they are not against us, they are for us." Who dares to suggest, asks Gunnel Vallquist, that these words would not take precedence over everything we give reference to when we persist in the division that keeps us from sharing the Lord's table in the fullness of unity?

11

So are there any signs in our time, that the prayer of Christ for unity in the Church ever will become visible? Yes and no.

The official work of ecumenism seems to have a hard time reaching further than polite conversations and non-binding documents. However, under the surface, there is an undertow growing more poignant. People are united in an underground movement, where talk about Christian unity is not all that prevalent as if it was a project to complete. One speaks more about the *unity in Christ,* and people are tasting the fruits of this growing reality.

Like the Coptic monastic father and visionary for unity, Matta al-Miskin, expressed it: "We must start by living together in the one and innermost being of faith before we can agree on the content." But, even for Father Matta, it is self-evident that *spiritual* unity needs to be revealed in *physical* expressions.

12

Is the visible unity of the church a realistic vision today? Or is it a dream, something that belongs in the heavenly realm? The subject requires that we once again pose the foundational questions: What constitutes a Christian church? How do we grow the fellowship of Christ? What does the path toward an "evangelical catholicity" look like? In other words, how can we that belong to the evangelical churches – the Lutheran and the Reformed as well as the later evangelical churches – be blessed by the treasure of faith contained in the worldwide church and, at the same time, serve the worldwide church with the gifts of our evangelical legacy for the sake of the unity of the church?

13

In the 19th century, when the Free Church movement began in Sweden, it was like runlets of renewal within the Swedish Lutheran Church (Church of Sweden). It is important to remember that the leading figures of this movement did not intend to start new churches; they wanted to see renewal and vitalization in the existing one.

This was true for Lewi Pethrus, who refused to secede from the Swedish Lutheran Church because he viewed the Pentecostal movement as a revival movement within the same. Martin Luther shared this viewpoint in the 16th century as well and, therefore, the same questions that are raised about free churches could also to a high degree be asked about the Lutheran Church, something that theologian Ola Tjørhom has done: "Given todays realities, can the Lutheran project be justified? Should it be sustained?"

In the same way that debaters from the Free Church, engaging the Swedish Lutheran Church in dialogue, do not intend that that they would become Lutherans, Tjørhom does not intend that Lutherans should become Roman Catholics. The question behind it all is greater: Is there a foundational continuity within the life of the church, spanning from the days of the apostles into our time, that suggests we share a common faith with the ones that have gone before us and, therefore, we do not need to "reinvent the wheel"? And, what does it mean as a Christian, as a church in Sweden today, to seek this continuity is upheld and not broken?

14

There may be reasons to pay attention to the similarities between the Lutheran Church and Free Church as movements of revival for different times. Maybe it will help us understand the crises that those two churches are facing today.

In contemporary, popular, historical science, Martin Luther has been portrayed as an anti-Catholic rebel that wanted to set the church free from Roman oppression. This portrait is historically deceptive. Luther viewed him-

self as a good Catholic, in fact, as a *better* Catholic than the church leaders he criticized. He had no intentions whatsoever to break away from Rome and form a new church but wanted to get rid of the misconduct that obscured the message of the gospel.

The same thing applies to the greater part of the Reformation as a whole during the first part of the 16th century. The purpose of the Reformation was to be correctional and, as such, a dynamic renewal within the one church. Every movement like this has had as its goal to make itself dispensable. The Reformation was deeply rooted in the heritage of the Catholic Church. The early creeds, like the Augsburg Confession, carry this awareness of continuity. This idea of continuity remained for a long time and was reflected in the words that Fredrika Bremer spoke to Pope Pius IX in 1859 when a cardinal said that a person like her should not have to die as a heretic. She answered, "But I am not a heretic. I am a catholic Christian." The cardinal answered, "But, not Roman Catholic?!"

"No," Bremer answered, "I consider myself more catholic than if I were so!"

15

As Christians in so-called Protestant countries, many of us grew up with a negative view of the very word catholic. When this word came into usage, already at the beginning of the 2nd century, it was not used as a confessional designation. The meaning of the word is "pertaining to the world as a whole" (a meaning many churches state in confessing the creed where the original wording is "I believe in the one, holy, catholic and apostolic Church").

No other word expresses that the Christian faith concerns everyone in all places in a more obvious and distinguished way. To confess the catholicity of the church is to confess her universality and wholeness.

Catholic is the opposite of provincial and opposes sectarianism even more. In this regard, the Orthodox Church has always viewed herself as catholic. After Luther and the Reformation, both Catholic and Protestant became confessional labels. Catholic meant Roman Catholic and Protestant became a negation of this. Since then, it is in this reality we find ourselves and as a consequence, many of us, understandably, feel uncomfortable when someone mentions that the church's identity always has been catholic.

16

Early in the 20th century this stance toward the catholicity of the church came into a renewed expression when church leaders like Nathan Söderblom and Manfred Björkqvist, not without resistance, spoke about the necessity of an 'evangelical catholicity' within the Lutheran Church of Sweden. Nathan Söderblom highlighted that, since the Reformation in Sweden, there is a foundational unity between the Lutheran Church of Sweden and the Roman Catholic Church bodies since no new church where created, unlike the ones in Germany and Denmark.

This catholic awareness deepened by the work of Father Gunnar Rosendahl and the liturgical renewal within the Lutheran Church of Sweden. It is beneficial to remember that the Lutheran Church of Sweden was not labeled "Lutheran" until the 18th century. The word

"Protestantism" only came into usage in the 19th century, and then only in a very limited way.

To be a "Catholic" church remained in the consciousness of the Lutheran Church of Sweden for centuries past the Reformation. The reformers didn't view the fracture with Rome as a betrayal of Catholicity. It was centuries later that one was labeled "not Catholic" if you called yourself a "Lutheran." Sven-Erik Brodd, an expert on Church history writes, "The Swedish Church became Protestant when the awareness of this designation overshadowed her consciousness to be a Catholic church."

17

There might be a connection between the alleged crises of the Free Church and her distinctive, prophetic identity. If this is the case, it's nothing to be ashamed of. On the contrary, the front figures of the Free Church revival, who constantly refused to call themselves "pastors," were not only preachers in the broad sense. They were prophets who testified in a way that pierced the hearts of people, contemporary equivalents to the ancient monks who refused to be ordained as priests.

The church withers without prophets. On a daily basis we need to pray that they will be sent our way and that we will recognize them when they show up, often unexpectedly. The mission of the prophets is not to plant and start new churches, it is rather to inspire the existing churches to be attentive and invite the wind of the Holy Spirit. When the prophets start to build and revival starts to organize new denominations, it runs the risk of shutting its adherents out from the width, the height and the depth of the rich deposit of faith within the church.

18

Just as all of Christianity needs the prophetic gift of the Spirit, it also requires a tradition for anchoring. Let us call it, «The Tradition of the Church.» It consists of the Holy Spirit's life-giving stream for 2,000 years of Christian history. It is deposited in the accumulated experience of spiritual life all the way back to the days of the apostles.

Tradition is not an addition to the scriptures and it does not superimpose itself over scriptures. Tradition is the incarnation of scriptures in the life of the Church. Tradition is the guarantor that Christianity nurtures the connection with her roots.

Tradition lends a perspective that lessens the risk for pride: we were not the first ones, we haven't gone the furthest and we do not possess the most knowledge. The ones that are asking if the Free Church has run its course, challenge us to an honest self-examination of our church identity. It is not without pain we do this and the questions cannot be answered lightly or quickly. To ask the questions may not be a betrayal of the heritage of the Free Church, but rather an expression of our duty to the original vision that the pioneers of the Free Church carried.

19

What does a renewed commitment to the tradition of the church imply for the Free Church? What does it mean for the Lutheran Church of Sweden?

A radical re-evaluation of the "Reformed" and the "Free Church" projects obviously does not mean that the Lutheran Church or the Free Churches cease to exist. The

discovery of the rich inheritance that we have received from the unified church must not allow us to forget, or even more importantly to despise, what we have received from the tradition we were born into. How can the original prophetic heritage from the Reformation and Free Church revivals serve the catholicity and unity of the church today?

20

For the Free Churches and the Lutheran Church of Sweden, a visible Christian unity must assume a form for expressing a fellowship with the bishop of Rome, the successor of Peter according to early tradition. We are not speaking about a unity under Rome, but with Rome. This can, of course, be applied to relations with Constantinople, Alexandria, Antioch and Moscow as mother churches within Orthodox Christianity as well, but I am primarily mentioning Rome here since it belongs to the western Christian hemisphere.

A fellowship like this assumes a mutual respect. If we from the younger churches could use a greater commitment toward the catholic and ecumenical ideals that distinguish the Christianity of the first millennium, the older churches, the Roman Catholic and the Orthodox, then those churches probably need the will to recognize the prophetic contribution to the church by the Evangelical and Reformed movements.

The way toward unity does not occur by conversion to each other's churches (although individuals sometimes feel called to this) and even less by one subduing the other. The way of Christ takes a different path: He is here among us, as the Servant of God's servants. The unity among His disciples that He prayed for will probably take us all by

surprise. Throughout the ages, the acts of the Holy Spirit seem to be identified by their surprising characteristics.

21

On December 8, 1965 – the same day as the conclusion of Vatican II – 23-year-old student Enzo Bianchi settled down in one of the houses on a ramshackle farm in Bose, in a hollow in a valley located below the nearly abandoned hamlet Magnano in Pimento, northern Italy. Some fifty years of constant presence by this one person have in this setting, with the Alps as a backdrop, created one of the most dynamic spiritual environments in Europe, and one of the most ecumenically radical as well.

Today Bose, together with Taize' are mentioned as perhaps the two most hopeful and important places of ecumenism in our part of the world. Both communities not only attract seeking and longing people from many different church backgrounds but have also garnered attention and respect among church leaders from all of Christianity.

Visitors from different parts of Christianity have found their way to Bose. In the Bose community, many of the brothers and sisters are Roman Catholics and have developed a strong bond with the Orthodox tradition. One of the many expressions of this is that all male novices in Bose get to spend a period of their noviciate at a monastery on Mount Athos.[3] Just in recent years, Bose has been

3 Mount Athos is a mountain and peninsula in northeastern Greece and an important centre of Eastern Orthodox monasticism. It is governed as an autonomous polity within the Greek Republic. Mount Athos is home to 20 monasteries under the direct jurisdiction of the Ecumenical Patriarch of Constantinople.

visited by the Orthodox patriarch Bartholomew and the Coptic Pope Tawadros, not to mention all the Italian bishops and priests who have come there for retreat, study and counsel. Former Anglican Archbishop Rowan Williams visits Bose regularly for personal retreats, and Pope Francis has highlighted this place as an example for monastic life and ecumenical approach in our time. The whole college of bishops from Sweden has traveled to Bose for retreat and the Pentecostal Theological Network has hosted days of reflection and deliberation there as well.

22

What was the reason behind Bose becoming an ecumenical community and a monastery where both men and women live together? "It was not planned," said Guido Dotti, who for many years has functioned as the vice prior alongside Enzo Bianchi.

The prayer group that brother Enzo belonged to as a student in Turin was ecumenical in nature, gathering in homes on a weekly basis to pray and read from the gospels. In the beginning, many were enthusiastic about finding a place where they could form a life in a community. Yet, when opportunity presented itself, no one had the courage to step out… except one.

Enzo Bianchi moved into the small farm by himself, without electricity or running water. For three years he lived in solitude, with the exception of the occasional friendly visit. He decided to thoroughly study the monastic traditions of both the west and the east.

During this time Bianchi got to know brother Roger and other brothers from the Taize' community - who at

the time belonged to the Reformed churches. He visited with Trappist monks in France and stayed for a month at the Greek Athonite State (Mount Athos) with the greatest concentration of monasteries in the Orthodox world.

23

Three years later, in 1968, three people joined Enzo Bianchi at Bose. One was a Reformed pastor from Switzerland; another a woman.

"There was no agenda or set rule," Dotti said. "That the community would become ecumenical and diverse, with both brothers and sisters, was a gift from God, something that came as a result of the personalities who sought brother Enzo out."

Maybe it was not surprising that the small group of 20-somethings and their community experiment were met with skepticism by the bishop of Biella, the diocese where Bose is located, and others. However, once Cardinal Michele Pellegrino of Turin, came to know the young adults in Bose, he quickly recognized they possessed energy and awareness the church needed.

"I take responsibility for these young people," cardinal Pellegrino told his fellow bishops in Northern Italy. Then and there, the young community came under the wings of the church and yet remained an autonomous fellowship, not subject the Roman Catholic Church or any other church for that matter, aligning with the pattern of how monasteries and communities since the 4th century have been functioning as an expression of the Church's prophetic charisma.

The encounter with the brothers and the sisters in Bose – their life, their hospitality, work, and worship – have been rejuvenating and clarifying for me. On a personal level, it has been purifying and corrective to listen, observe, converse and form fresh ideas. It is, simply put, an encounter with a way of life that leaves a lasting impression.

By the fruit you will recognize the tree: this is the eternal rule of discernment put forward in the gospel.[4] The trademark of healthy spiritual environments, ecumenically genuine in their character, is that individuals from very different backgrounds all feel welcome. It is not necessary to belong to a certain part of the church with a designated theological etiquette to feel at ease.

In Bose and Taize', people who would rarely visit the same conferences and meetings, get to know one another, without pretense. Today, Monstero de Bose is a small, vibrant society with publishing, carpentry, bakery, pottery, iconography, marmalade and candle manufacturing and impressive gardens where tomatoes, squash and kale are cultivated side by side. Everything is clean and well-organized; work is done meticulously and with great care. Since 1999, the church of the monastery points towards the sky at the centre of this "society," its bells calling the community to prayer three times a day.

The convergence of old and new marks this place. This is true of the art that meets the visitor as well: traditional iconography and modern art in an appealing blend. The motto from Vatican II *nobilitas simplicitas* – noble

4 Matt 7:20

simplicity – functions as guide. The harmony of beauty and simplicity is embodied in the architecture as well.

25

Yet it is not the exterior surface that leaves the strongest impression among the visitors of Bose, rather the encounters with the people who live there. If the temptation of exclusivity and elitism lurks behind every Christian experiment keen to adhere to the original ideals of the gospel, it might be particularly true in regard to the cloistered life. People living in monasteries and convents, traditionally speak about their own vocation as a "consecration," that is to say, a holy life. What does that imply for other vocations, such as matrimony? From the beginning of Bose, Enzo Bianchi chose not to use such exclusionary language.

"There is only one consecrating action in the Christian life. It is baptism," Bianchi emphatically states. "In being baptized and set apart for God we all have different vocations to fulfill and to be faithful toward. No way of life is more holy than another."

An evident example of this is that, although they lead a traditional life of celibacy, the brothers and sisters of Bose refrain from wearing monastic vesture. The only hint in that direction is the white albs worn in worship. In day-to-day life, everyone wears their own clothes.

While the brothers and sisters have sequestered living quarters in one part of the monastery, they welcome tens of thousands of guests each year. They spend time together and with guests in a natural, transparent and relaxed way. Brother Matteo emphasizes this as he guides visitors

around the monastery: “We don’t use the word ‘cloistered,’ since that does not describe the reality of our life.”

26

It is hard to find a more clear example of an ecumenical posture than what meets the visitor at Bose. All who are baptized are invited to the Lord’s table. This eucharistic hospitality is significant in its own right when keeping in mind that the mass is celebrated in the Roman order and the majority of the brothers and sisters are Roman Catholic. However, you can find this practice in many places around Europe.

The greatest testimony is that the community *is* and *remains* ecumenical. When Enzo Bianchi, himself a Roman Catholic, receives people from other churches who wish to enter the community, he advises against converting to Roman Catholicism. Each and every one who becomes a member of this community remains faithful to the church in which they were planted.

This is ultimately manifested when the monastic vows are professed. When a person who is entering into the monastery takes the final vows, he or she is also received on location by a person from their own church: a Roman Catholic bishop for those of Roman Catholic faith, a Reformed pastor if Lutheran and a Pentecostal pastor for the Pentecostal. Talk about taking steps on the road toward unity.

The Vatican is fully aware of Enzo Bianchi’s progressive ecumenical posture. The fact that Pope Francis entrusted him as his personal advisor in ecumenical questions speaks volumes. Far from all Roman Catholics,

maybe not even the pope, insist today that the way toward the church's visible unity consists of Christians in other churches converting to Rome. While individuals from different faiths may choose to convert, ecumenical reasons for conversion must be questioned.

27

Incarnating a spirit of unity must be about more than dialogue and strategies. Even the pastoral motive is not the deepest one.

All unity finds its source and motivation in the great mystery of the Trinity. As we proceed into this mystery, the harder it is to live separated from our brothers and sisters in the worldwide church. Unity becomes a convicting necessity.

How do we know we are on the right track? Let's look to Isaac the Syrian as our guide. He belonged to the eastern Syrian church, sometimes called "Nestorian," that had been banned from the Byzantine Christian empire. Isaac reached beyond the established lines of division and his writings spread far beyond his own tradition. Even in places of conflict, it was not unusual that Isaac's teachings were read on both sides of the fence. His teachings are seasoned with strong emphases on humility, self-emptying, patience and mercy – absolutely foundational characteristics for living a holy and spiritually healthy life.

Isaac did not have any problem finding inspiration from traditions that seemed very different from one another. He was nourished by spiritual leaders who had been condemned by the councils of the church. Isaac has

been called a mystic, but that does not find its expression in elaborate stories concerning his own spiritual experiences.

"No," Samuel Rubenson ascertains in the small essay *Landet där tankarna funnit ro* (*The Country Where Thoughts Are at Peace*), "...rather it is from the viewpoint that Isaac, like a focused prism, manages to catch and become one with the full spiritual tradition that we only get to see every once in a while."

28

Isaac the Syrian is an ecumenical forerunner because he understood why, and in what way, love for our enemies is the sharp sword of the gospel. A short excerpt from his spiritual writings illustrates the contours of the posture every Christian is called to seek when conflicts between peoples and persons arise:

"When you meet your neighbour, force yourself to pay him more honour than may be his due: kiss his hand and his foot, make your heart fervent with a holy love for him, grasp his hands time and time again, placing them on your eyes and caressing them with great honour. Attribute to his person all sorts of virtues, even if they may not apply to him. And when he is absent, speak good and noble things of him. Address him in respectful terms. In this sort of way, not only will you impel him to desire these virtues (since he will be ashamed of the undeserved reputation with which you credit him) and sow in him the seed of good deeds, but you will also find that, by habituating yourself in this way, you will establish in yourself gentle and humble manners, and you will be freed from

many tiresome struggles, against the likes of which others have to guard themselves by constant labours."

29

Gregory of Nyssa, one of the most influential spiritual teachers of the 4th century, confronted early tendencies of so-called individualism when he expressed rather playfully that there is not "individuals" like some people would suggest, but rather "one humanity." "Don't fribble with the language", Gregory exclaims. Things become to us what we say about them. It is a linguistic mistake to use expressions like "individuals" or "independent". Gregory's writings illustrate how we are indeed a diverse community that shares in the same human nature, but in every one of us the nature of man is the same and therefore one. Strictly speaking there is only *one* person, something Paul already mentioned when speaking about the church as "one body."[5]

Deepening this understanding, this paradigm, concerning the nature of man, one of the first millennium's most brilliant theologians in the church, Maximos the Confessor, who lived in the 7th century, summarized a vision about man and church that involves the whole cosmos. For Maximos, as well as other church fathers, the point of departure is God's Trinitarian life. The Holy Trinity is not an abstract theological principle. It reveals God a person, not a solitary. It makes man into mankind, rather than isolated individuals.

The concept of the person contains a key for a Christian understanding of God and man. The convic-

5 Eph 4:4

tion that the Divine nature consists of a dynamic dance between the Father, the Son and the Holy Spirit is the essence of the faith in the unified church. But all logic fails when it attempts to grasp this secret: the digit three in the Trinity is not a number.

"God, Who is beyond everything, is worshiped by us as Trinity and as One Godhead, yet He is not three or one in the way we are acquainted with these numbers," says Maximos.

The divine persons cannot be summarized. The Father is in the Son and the Son in the Father and the Spirit proceeds from the Father in fellowship with the Son. God is the eternal, cosmic dance, called *perichoresis* by the fathers. The essential meaning of this is that the nature of God is love. And also, that man, created in the image of God, by nature is love!

Love requires the other. It takes two to love. If God the Father was alone, how could he be love? If God was the Son on his own, who could He share his love with before the beginning of time? No, God is the Father Who loved the Son, rejoiced in the Spirit and invited mankind, created in the image of God, into the community that lasts for eternity. In this way, the doctrine of the Trinity reveals God as a Person, and not some distant, enigmatic spirit.

Christian faith is more than the notion of a presence; it is the encounter with a Person. It is this encounter that leads to a radical conversion from all individualism because it makes us appear as unique and distinguished persons who share in humanity with all other persons. As little as the Father can be imagined without the Son and the Holy Spirit, man cannot be imagined without mankind and the Christian without the church.

30

One cannot help but ponder to what extent individualism – and therefore the division that reigns in our culture and parts of the church – finds its footing in the loss of a Trinitarian vision of God. Everything was about relationship for Maximos the Confessor. The fall in the Garden of Eden he describes in terms of falling from a person to an individual. Evil strikes mankind in three blows: first, isolation from the Source of creation, then a self-centred focus attempting to control the image. The third strike of evil is that our relationship with our neighbour develops into tyranny. The fall strikes at all of our relationships.

The incarnation is the foundation of our salvation, Maximos continues. In Christ, humanity and divinity enter a *relationship* and therefore the same thing may occur in every single person, indeed in all of creation. Just like Christ, it is a movement in two directions: toward God and toward the world. Salvation is the transformative process that fulfills everything that was planted in humankind created in the image of God. Through the process of salvation, relationships begin to heal so that we can become *more of a* person, but never *more than a* person.

31

Maximos outlook concerning humankind and creation-theology is one of the grandest views encountered in the first millennium of the church. Proceeding from God's unity in trinity, he views mankind's unity by diversity. As an image of God, mankind is one, yet simultaneously a composite of spirit, soul and body, reflecting the whole

cosmos in its diversity. Humanity is the world in miniature, a microcosm, with the vocation of being a mediator between creation and its Creator.

Maximos maintains that mankind participates in the life of God as a part of the church. Our relation to God cannot be imagined outside the life of the church, which is an image of both God and humanity. The church testifies about the incarnation: heaven and earth, divinity and humanity, are unified in the church. As "the body of Christ" the church represents the whole world as well as the Godhead. She stands in the service of reconciliation between Creator and creation.

"The church is man and man is church," Maximos summarizes. The vision is breathtaking and challenging: it is only when the church is *one* that she becomes heaven on earth.

32

Some encounters reveal our character. Are we capable of embracing the ones we live separated from with tender and loving prayer, regardless of if that separation is because of them turning away from relationship or our inability to understand them?

Separation is a wound – in us and in the other. The purpose of unity and the foundation of an ecumenical posture is to "heal the wounds of others by accepting it as ours" like Chiara Lubich was known to say. What does it mean to accept the brokenness of others as our own? It means that we must always aim to begin from the other person's experiences, tradition, theology and horizon. To receive the other is to receive this person's questions,

doubts and criticisms in earnestness. We must discern ourselves in light of these things before we put forward our own contribution. We shelve the arguments, realizing the path to unity is not to say, “You are wrong, and I am right,” nor to say, “You are right,” for the sake of unity if that means we hide the things that actually separate us.

Before we can converge in the things that separate us in regard to the content of our faith, we need to know every experience that hurts the other like our own, beginning with the other’s way of thinking. This is not denying the convictions we confess based on the foundation of Christ and the scriptures, but rather seeking any light we might receive from another viewpoint so that we might understand ourselves and our faith more clearly.

33

“Divisions among Christians are a scandal. There is no other word for it: a scandal!” These words are from Pope Francis, uttered during an audience in Rome in 2015. In a prophetic and very challenging way, he exhorted his listeners to ask themselves how they might grow in their faith by receiving the light of the Holy Spirit through other churches than their own. The bishop of Rome encourages us “to find in other Christians something which we need, something which we could receive as a gift from our brothers and sisters.”

34

Hopefully, all Christians can sign off on Jesus’s words about loving your neighbour as yourself. But, another

question carries the same kind of weight: What does it mean to love my neighbour's church as well as my own? Can the Pentecostal see the Roman Catholic as someone who may enrich their own faith experience? Can the Roman Catholic see the Pentecostal in this light? If that is the case, we cannot distance ourselves from each other any longer.

Naturally, this will require great efforts and attentive listening. Above all, it presumes a great respect for the Holy Spirit, Who blows where He wills and uses who He wills when He wills.

Before we reach this point of impartial listening we have to leave all our prestige, all our pride and all our self-defense with the abandoned Christ on the cross. Every church needs to die to its own ego as well.

But sometimes we can also become fascinated and tantalized by the treasures we have found in other traditions, and we may need to ask the question in a different way: what does it mean to love *my own church* as well as my neighbours? It can become a challenge to faithfully remain where you are when you think your own church has not shown considerable understanding for what you may have found enriching in encounters with other Christians. It can be even more challenging if you feel you're own church is not faithful to the gospel in the way you interpret it.

There may be instances when someone clearly finds a home in a different tradition and church, and the wisest thing to do is to affirm this. However, a fruitful ecumenical pursuit assumes just as often – probably more often – that we continue to work for the unity of the church from the tradition in which we were baptized. This can be to walk the way of the cross as well.

35

A gripping, radical and admirable example of a cross-like ecumenical demeanour was formed by Roman Catholic Bishop Klaus Hemmerle (1929 - 1994). Among other things, he was the initiator of the annual ecumenical council of bishops that still takes place on the initiative of the Focolare movement. The ones that knew him described him as a person "in love with the Word of God." For Hemmerle, the Word of God was the foundation for all dialogue. He always attempted to begin with scriptures as well as rediscover scriptures through the contributions of others.

He emphasized concepts like *sola scriptura* and *sola gratia* with such ardor that these typically Protestant expressions took on a whole new meaning for many Roman Catholics. To Hemmerle, expressions like these were not divisive. He would say, "My evangelical brothers, with their passion for living the Word, have given back my Catholic identity in a new way."

Hemmerle's ecumenical style was not to simply settle for compromise or to meet half way by joining a piece of one tradition with another's. His reliance on the Holy Spirit was astonishing. Because of this trust, he could say to the people in other churches, "I'm not leaving you before I see the gifts of the Holy Spirit in you."

He refused to let go of the thought that Christ is present and active in every person, even in the one with a different confession, even in a fellowship that has separated themselves from the church. "I admire Jesus, Who is present in each and every one of us," Hemmerle could say.

The consequence of this conviction was also clear. "If I am not prepared to receive God where He is present, if I'm not loving God in my brother who belongs to a church separate from mine but rather avoid the way of pain, confrontation, love and uncertainty, then I am not saying a real yes to God." For Klaus Hemmerle this choice was necessary: to say yes to Christ, Who lives in the midst of the brothers and sisters in the churches you have been separated from.

36

Such is the way of the cross, and Hemmerle could not see any other possible way for the divided churches to be unified. Jesus carries all evil upon the cross and transforms it by exposing Himself in the utmost sacrificial vulnerability.

"The quickest way to Jesus's presence in our midst among the churches does not come by us avoiding the things that separate us or from us forcefully trying to fit pieces that do not fit together, nor by concessions or compromises, but by us saying yes to the crucified One," Hemmerle said. He meant that the things that separate us then become the key toward unity. The things that hurt us become the gateway to joy.

The path that Klaus Hemmerle advocates, and that he himself was an example of, does not replace tedious theological work. Rather, it makes theological work possible, but from a different paradigm. The way of mutual love begets a stance that unites two seemingly irreconcilable approaches: considering the other perspective as one's own and using it as the starting point while at the same time keeping a "crystal clear allegiance towards your own

church's theology." This way is not about pinning one opinion against another, but about exhausting every effort in trying to understand why the other thinks and believes the way he or she does. The goal is that we would, at last, be able to give the gift of the Holy Spirit to each other so that through them we may find the one and deep fountain of unity, the unity reflected in the Holy Trinity.

37

One of the people who lived and testified about this unity, always with unshakable faithfulness towards her own church, was Gunnel Vallquist. As a young girl, she was received in the Roman Catholic Church, but later in life, she came to enjoy the interaction with the Orthodox tradition more and more, the liturgy in particular. However, Vallquist never considered leaving her own church.

While remaining a Roman Catholic, at the end of her life she came to enter "full communion" with the Orthodox Church. For many years Gunnel Vallquist traveled to Paris during Great Lent to participate in the Orthodox liturgy in a couple of churches that she returned to. She testifies about a "breakthrough" that came to mean a lot for her personally. "I suffered through, and was well aware of, the strict impossibility that I, as a non-Orthodox, could participate in the eucharist," she said. "But one day, November 5, 2000, in the crypt of the cathedral at Rue Daru, when Father Boris Bobrinsky (whom I have gotten to know when he visited Sweden in 1988 and after that confided with once a year when I've arrived in Paris) was presiding, I suddenly felt that I had to ask permission. It was during communion itself. I stood up in the line and

when I met the gaze of Father Boris, my facial expression conveyed a question for him. He bowed his head a little and I could proceed. This was a defining day in my life. Every year since then, I have been welcome to receive the eucharist when he was presiding.

"After a couple of years, I asked him if when I visit other Orthodox churches I can tell them that I am Orthodox. He thought for a while and then said, 'Je vais vous recevoir dans l'Eglise Orthodox.' ('I will receive you into the Orthodox Church.')

"My immediate reply was, 'It is impossible for me to leave the Catholic Church.' He said, 'Il 'en est pas question.' ('It is not about that.')

"This was, of course, an unusual situation – not totally unique, but decidedly non-canonical. Archbishop Gabriel, who was informed about the situation, permitted it but emphasized that it could not be known.

"I've shared my secret with a few close friends; no one has seemed shocked. The priests I've spoken to have wished me good fortune. And, I am of good fortune. After so many years of writing and speaking about how the work of unity should begin at the Lord's table, rather than the other way around, I find myself in a situation where the walls of division have been torn down."

38

What Gunnel Vallquist called her "Orthodox orientation" began already in the 1950s. It was during a phase when her own church was heading toward Vatican II and, as she expresses it, "the ecumenical movement had oriented its vision toward the undivided church, theology made its

way through and beyond all additions and splinters and found its way back to the sources, to the first centuries of Christian faith and praxis." She testified about how Orthodoxy increasingly became "the spring where the innermost part of my soul may drink, the language that reaches the deepest places of my heart."

Vallquist did not want to broadcast or take advantage of the fact that she was received to live in full communion with the Orthodox Church. A couple of years before her death, as she gave me one of the last pieces she wrote – a longer article – about this experience, she said she wanted to share her testimony. But, she requested, "wait until after I die."

What consequences did Gunnel Vallquist's fellowship with the Orthodox Church have for her Catholic identity? She writes, "This pickle of a situation took a long time for me to integrate. Now I am able to express that I am Catholic in an almost physical way; I am a member of the Catholic Church like one is a member of a family. She is my natural homestead, like my physical family, if you could say such a thing about a religion."

39

Gunnel Vallquist's testimony about her "new pickle of a situation," is a divine wink pointing to a path that the Holy Spirit can open, beyond the limitations and prejudices that tradition in the "horizontal" way easily creates. It is not by forcefully attempting to remove the blockades, claiming our own right or taking things into our own hands.

Unconventional ecumenical initiatives, such as when Wilfred Stinissen invited non-Roman Catholics to the eucharistic table during an ecumenical retreat, presupposes a communal affirmation. It is a mutual self-emptying founded on empathic recognition.

The Orthodox theologian Vladimir Lossky reflects on the distinction between tradition's vertical and horizontal sides. Tradition in a vertical sense nurtures the connection with the original sources. It is not the messenger of truth says Lossky, but the light that reveals the truth.

Traditions in the horizontal sense, on the other hand, can become a great obstacle for us to encounter the Holy Spirit. How do we know that the Spirit is doing something new, or that the new is just another sidetrack or even disillusion? Discernment is a delicate task. The risk for presumptuousness is always present when we are attempting to discern what traditions reflect the light of the Holy Spirit and what traditions we need to leave behind.

40

It is 7 a.m. on April 19, 2016. I am part of a small gathering of people who have been invited to Casa di Santa Marta in the Vatican to celebrate mass at the house chapel of Pope Francis. (One of the first initiatives Pope Francis instated when elected bishop of Rome and leader of the Roman Catholic Church in March 2013 was the decision not to reside in the private apartment where popes for many generations have lived during their pontificate, but rather in a guest house in the Vatican. The house, known as Santa Marta, is located obliquely behind the church of Peter.)

As we enter the Vatican at 6.30 a.m., we go through several security checkpoints where members of the pope's security detail and Italian military police, *Carabinieri*, make sure our names are on the list of invited guests. When we arrive at Santa Marta we are guided to a reception area to wait for a couple of minutes before we are led into the chapel. The lighting is dimmed, the altar is resting in light, above the words: *Veni Sancte Spiritus*, "Holy Spirit, come."

The homily of the pope this morning will touch upon how to be brave and receive the new things that the Spirit is doing. A small congregation of about 30 people finds its place in the simply designed but beautiful chapel. Everything is quiet and refreshingly void of mobile cameras and other trivialities that are often present when the bishop of Rome appears. Pope Francis enters the chapel through a side entrance, he bows lightly, first toward the tabernacle, then towards the altar. Matter-of-factly and very quietly, as is his habit, he leads the early-morning mass with a seemingly undisturbed presence. Many that have met this spiritual father testify about his ability to always be present in the moment, with the people he meets and in the event that is taking place.

41

"The Lord be with you," Pope Francis greets us in the beginning of the mass. "And with your Spirit," we all reply.

The homily during these morning masses in the Santa Marta house is a special experience. The pope preaches in a conversational style and tone without notes. It is as though he is sitting at the end of a table and is engaging in a dialogue with whoever is there. The tone and gestures may change,

but he never raises his voice. There is complete absence of sermon mannerisms and rhetorical tricks. Today the gospel passage is from John, chapter 10; the epistle is from Acts. Jesus is teaching about the shepherd and the sheep is, about open or closed hearts. Do we, like Barnabas in Acts, dare to "accept the new and not shut your heart because of suspicion" Pope Francis points out in his homily. "A heart that remains open to God can receive the new things that the Holy Spirit is doing," says the bishop of Rome.

After the homily, we remain quiet in reflection and prayer before the mass continues with the celebration of the eucharist; the meal that makes the church present in her fullness. We receive the body and blood and linger in the satisfying silence. With the blessing of the Lord, Pope Francis sends us out into the world to follow Christ, open to the new things that the Spirit is doing.

But, before I leave, Pope Francis meets me outside the small chapel of Santa Marta.

"Ah, you are from Sweden! I will visit you in the fall. October I believe," he says to me.

"Yes, that's right," I say. "The end of October. A warm welcome awaits you." I explain that I am a Pentecostal pastor and belong to an ecumenical community in Sweden, and I thank him for everything he is doing for Christian unity.

"I know that unity is very close to your heart," I say.

Pope Francis looks at me with his steady, fatherly gaze. Then he says with great emphasis,

"We must walk together!"

WE MUST WALK TOGETHER. We have to overcome the divisions and tear down the walls. That is one of our most important tasks today, says the bishop of Rome, the Francis of our time.

II. An Ecumenical Perspective Concerning the Office of Peter

1

I'm reading two collections of letters. One collection is written by Bishop Ignatius to the seven young churches in the generation succeeding the apostles. The other collection consists of a selection of correspondence from the writings of Lewi Pethrus that was published a couple of years ago under the title, *The Letters of Lewi.* Despite the fact that the collections are separated by 1,800 years, they strike a similar vein.

These letters are written as a response to a situation, as is often the case with letters like these. Conflicts, fragmentation and heresies motivates the authors to reach for the ink. To a great degree, this is also true about the letters of the New Testament.

Ignatius writes to congregations that were started by the apostles or their fellow workers, of which many were not past their teenage years. Lewi Pethrus letters are written at a time when the "honeymoon stage" is over and early signs of sickness are starting to show within the movement of which he is the natural leader.

For both authors the question of unity is essential. They notice how divisive teachings, exaggerations and power-seeking individuals threaten the peace within and between congregations. They appeal and they exhort, correct and teach, for the sake of maintaining unity. Repeatedly, Ignatius highlights the bishop as the guardian of unity in the congregations. Lewi Pethrus practices an office for unity in his person in a movement that's bending and breaking and might at any moment be ripped apart.

2

At the end of the 1st century, Ignatius was the bishop in Antioch in the Northern part of Syria, in the congregation whose beginning is recorded in the 11th chapter of Acts. He is considered one of the apostolic fathers, a designation that is often used about the early church leaders in the generation after the apostles. Many of them had been taught at the feet of Peter, John, Paul or another of the twelve. Their leadership safeguarded that there was continuity with the time of the apostles and, therefore, with Jesus Himself.

Ignatius entered his office as bishop (from Greek "*episkopos,*" translated in the New Testament as "overseer") around 70 AD, around the same time as Luke writes the *Acts of the Apostles.* He oversees the church in Antioch for about thirty years.

Sometime during the reign of Emperor Trajan (98 – 117 AD), he is sentenced to be executed and is escorted by soldiers from Antioch to Rome where he is thrown to the wild beasts of the newly built Colosseum. During the journey toward his own death, Ignatius writes seven letters. Six of them he directs to different congregations, and one letter he sends to his fellow bishop in Smyrna, Polycarp, who received instruction from John the apostle.

It is a unique collection of letters, the oldest preserved within Christianity on this side of the New Testament. The letters are filled with the fiery faith that was so distinguishing for the early Church. Jesus, the Christ, true God and true man, is found at the centre of Ignatius' life and purpose. In his letters, two things are repeated again and again as determinants for the unity in Christ: faithfulness

toward the bishop as to God Himself and the peace in communion around the eucharistic table. The celebration of the eucharist is a confirmation of Christ Who became flesh and a rejection of the heresies that denied that Christ came in the flesh and remains present in the bread.

3

Through his letters, Ignatius provides a unique glimpse into the leadership structure that seems to be present in all of his contemporary's congregations: the bishop (the overseer) led the congregation together with the presbyters (the elders) and the deacons (the servants of the congregation). The nucleus to this threefold office is already found in the New Testament, but now it has been given an articulated foundation in the inner life of the congregation's organization.

The reason for this is obvious for the ones reading the letters of Ignatius. Without defined roles in leadership, anchored in the order that can be traced back to the apostles as well as the local congregation (and because of that, affirmed by the college of bishops), it becomes difficult, if not impossible, to keep the unity of the church over time.

Ignatius calls the church to respect the bishop as "a copy of the Father" in his letter to the Trallians and to respect the presbyters as "the council of God and the band of the apostles." Time and time again Ignatius exhorts the churches to do "nothing apart from the bishop." In his letter to the Ephesians he writes, "Wherefore it is fitting that you should run together in accordance with the will of your bishop, which thing also you do. For your justly

renowned presbytery, worthy of God, is fitted as exactly to the bishop as the strings are to the harp."[6]

4

We find the praxis that contributed to the unity between churches as early as the 1st century. When a church elected a new bishop, bishops from three nearby churches would participate in the liturgy where the new bishop was installed into office. This praxis created a collegiality between the bishops of the different churches, as well as preventing tendencies toward isolation and conflicts between different churches. When a crisis that didn't seem to have a solution broke out within a church, there were ties to bishops in other churches that could mediate and assist.

The principle that every congregation is autonomous, at the same time as not being self-sufficient, was important at this time in church history. This precept grew from the belief that Christ's body is One and undivided in its local and catholic expression. At the same time as every local congregation was considered to manifest the fullness of Christ's body, the same congregation could not be thought of as complete aside from the catholic expression of all congregations. A congregation in a designated location is not only a *part* of the universal church; every congregation is also called to manifest the fullness of the "one, holy and apostolic Church" as the creed from Nicaea and Constantinople proclaims.

6 St. Ignatius letter to the Ephesians is a part of *The Apostolic Fathers*

The Church is one, in every location and in the whole world, because Christ is One. If she fails to live in unity she will display a broken Christ to the world – a world that will then be hindered to believe. The foundation of this view is found in the words of Jesus in the high priestly prayer He prays facing His passion, "That all of them may be one, Father, just as You are in Me and I am in You. May they also be in Us so that the world may believe that You have sent Me."[7]

5

In the early church, the understanding of church ecclesiology was first and foremost shaped by the view that the church was the body of Christ. John Chrysostom says, "There is no separation between the head and the body, the slightest separation would destroy us."

"Under the breath and fire of the Spirit, there exists in Christ a single human Being in a multitude of persons: the body of Christ in which we are all 'members of one another'", writes Olivier Clément. This transforms the church into a sacrament, or as the Eastern Church would express it, a mystery. The heart in this sacramental reality is the eucharist, "the mystery of mysteries." It is the eucharist that constitutes the church as the body of Christ. It is not in a magical way that the church owns Christ or *is* Christ, but only by the descent and presence of the Holy Spirit.

Every sacramental reality assumes what in liturgical language is called *epiclesis,* a supplication for the Holy

7 John 17:21

Spirit to be poured out so that the church may be a continuous Pentecost. Olivier Clément states that "it is the epiclesis that allows for the universal priesthood of every believer, and that of the ordained priesthood with bishops and presbyters, to reach its full expression." All faithful participate in the supplication for the presence of the Holy Spirit as "temples of the living God." Clément paints a picture of how the laity have a purifying and preventative effect on the bishops of the church: "When it is needed, they call them back to their original purpose."

6

When threats against the faith and unity of the church became evident, the bishops began to congregate to deliberate and discern a common way forward that remained true to the apostolic deposit of faith. When the shepherds of the congregations stood together, they were able to withstand heresies and dividing tendencies. Every bishop of the young church had a two - fold responsibility: he was to lead and keep the unity of a local congregation, and he was to testify to the catholicity of the worldwide church through his communion with the other bishops. These two tasks were inseparable; every congregation had a responsibility to maintain the local fellowship as well as the communion with other congregations. The body of Christ is always one.

It was natural that the bishops from the bigger cities would speak with greater authority at these councils. By the mandate they possessed representing the bigger congregations, their word and testimony often staked out the way ahead. Three congregations distinguished themselves early in Christianity: the churches in Antioch, Alexandria and

Rome. During the 4th century a fourth church was added to this list of influential churches: Constantinople. This occurred as a result of the empire's capital being moved from Rome to Bysans, the city located at the narrow strait of the Bosporus and named after the emperor of the time.

At the same time, Jerusalem regained its status as one of the main churches. A host of new churches were built there in the 4th century, including the basilica that would become one of the most important in Christianity: *Anastasia,* the holy Sepulchre, built on the location where the cross of Jesus Christ was re-discovered. With Jerusalem, the leading quartet of churches became a quintet.

7

The mother church was located in Jerusalem, and when this church reached its peak, it had tens of thousands of members.[8] But, it would be subject to a devastating blow when Emperor Titus' war machine sacked the city and plundered the temple in 70 AD. Antioch then increased in prominence: both Paul and Peter had ministered in this Syrian congregation. The church in Alexandria claimed it had ties to Peter as well, being founded by a disciple of the same, Mark.

Already during the second generation after the apostles, Rome came to take a distinct position. The church in the imperial capital testified about the victory of the gospel in the power centre of the ancient world. Of great importance was also that both Paul and Peter, the two great apostles had come here and, according to early Christian tradition, given up their lives as martyrs.

8 Acts 21:20

A generation later, Ireaneus of Lyon speaks about how Rome had a designated function, a *charisma,* that concerned the full unity of the church. "The great church, the best known and the most ancient of all churches, founded and constituted by the two glorious apostles Peter and Paul… For it is a matter of necessity that every Church should agree with this Church," he said. Because of this, it was only natural that the bishop of Rome had a designated position in the episcopal college of bishops. His office was not more important than the other bishops, but he was the first among equals (*primus inter pares*). The weight of the responsibility for the unity of the Church fell on his shoulders in an particular way. The shepherd for the church in Rome was the successor of Peter, the disciple whom Jesus had given a special responsibility in the great commission event recorded in the New Testament.[9] With Jesus's affirmation of Peter to be a shepherd for the sheep, and to "strengthen your brothers," came a commission that encompassed the unity of the young church.

8

The unique position that Peter grew into among the twelve disciples is highlighted in the gospels time after time. Peter's name is always mentioned first when the apostles are listed. We read, "And Simon and those who were with him."[10] Or at Pentecost: "But Peter, standing up with the eleven."[11] And later: "Peter and the rest of the apostles."[12]

---

9 John 21:15 - 19
10 Mark 1:36
11 Acts 2:14
12 Acts 2:37

He is the first one to confess Jesus to be the Messiah and the first of the apostles to meet the risen Christ. It is Peter that discerns the events during Pentecost and he emerges as the given spokesperson for the church in Jerusalem.

The description of Peter as being the first among the apostles does not mean that he has a higher authority, rather a special *charisma* among the ones who have been given the same mission and mandate. Peter does not have veto in the college of apostles. His words carry much weight in the important Jerusalem council:[13] he speaks first, but his words do not dictate the outcome.

There is a foundational sense of consensus among the "apostles and elders, with the whole church"[14] behind the decision that eventually transpires. Neither does his task of "strengthen your brothers" mean that it is him that legitimizes their office, Christ does.

9

Peter's role as a leader among the apostles is based upon the following three remarks by Jesus.

- "And I also say to you that you are Peter and on this rock I will build My church."[15]
- "And when you have returned to Me, strengthen your brothers."[16]
- "Simon… do you love Me more than these?"[17]

---

13 Acts 15:22 - 29
14 Acts 15:23
15 Matt 16:18
16 Luke 22:32
17 John 21:15

The first point to point out is that all three statements connects the Eucharist with the resurrection. According to the tradition of the early church (Ignatius of Antioch), it is the authentic celebration of the eucharist that is the prime event for shaping the foundation for the ecclesiality of the local church and makes her able to be in communion with all other churches.

However, two of these remarks are immediately followed by stern warnings from Jesus. When, on the basis of Peter's confession of faith, Jesus establishes him as "the rock" on which He will build His church, Peter refuses to accept that this Messiah, whom he has just proclaimed, is identical with the suffering servant. Whereupon Jesus flings at him: "Get behind Me, Satan! You are an offense to Me, for you are not mindful of the things of God but the things of men."[18]

And, when Jesus says to Peter, "I have prayed for you that your faith should not fail; and when you have returned to Me, strengthen your brethren," Peter exclaims that he is prepared to share the same fate as his Master. Jesus answers, "I tell you, Peter, the rooster shall not crow this day before you deny three times that you know Me."[19]

The third remark, at the end of the gospel of John, reveals that Peter must become, in the words of Olivier Clément, "the very example of the pardoned sinner" if he is going to be able to remain faithful to his calling. After reinstating Peter as the first among the apostles – "Do you love me more than these?" – the Lord exhorts him once more and promises nothing more than martyrdom. "But

18 Matt 16:23
19 Luke 22:34

when you are old, you will stretch out your hands, and another will gird and carry you where you do not wish."[20]

Peter's designated role in the church has no connection with worldly power and glory whatsoever. Peter, through his life and testimony, stands as a reminder that the church draws it's life from God's forgiveness and has no other power than that of a cross. Jesus candidly emphasized this point about Christian leadership when he said, "He who is greatest among you, let him be as the younger, and he who governs, as he who serves."[21]

10

The role that Peter receives from Jesus presents an archetype for institutional leadership within the church, that which came to be performed by the bishops and their colleges, the presbyters or the elders. In the same way, Paul's mission is an icon of the charismatic leadership in the church. He is the example that mercy sometimes circumvents the established order.

Paul was called to be an apostle without fulfilling the criteria for apostleship stipulated by Peter in his sermon in the first chapter of Acts, which was to have witnessed the events of Jesus from the baptism in Jordan to the ascension on the Mount of Olives.[22] The institutional and the charismatic dimensions are equally necessary within the church. Order and liberty are mutually dependent on each other. On rare and joyous occasions, it so happens that they converge. When bishops are anointed with the

20 John 21:18
21 Luke 22:26
22 Acts 1:21 - 22

gift of prophesy, something that can be said about Peter, the church emerges with clarity as the body of Christ in the world.

11

The bishop was the shepherd and the overseer of the local congregation in the early church. The structure from episcopal churches that we are familiar with today, with bishops appointed over dioceses, is something that develops within the church much later. Initially, every bishop is responsible for his own congregation at the same time as he is responsible for the relationship with other congregations.

The office of the bishop, or the overseer, is in one way always the "Office of Peter." It is the task of the bishop to guard the confession of Jesus as God's Son, to support and strengthen his colleges in their struggle to protect the flock and to lay down his life for the sheep. No one carries this burden to the same extent as the one who is called "first among equals."

The bishops in the prominent cities with big congregations naturally grew into this responsibility, particularly, the bishop who led the church in the city where Peter and Paul, the first and the last of the apostles, had laid down their lives down for the sheep. Rome, as the capital of the empire, was the centre for all kinds of idolatry: "Babylon, the great, the mother of harlots and of the abominations of the earth."[23] There, more than anywhere else, the gospel of Christ's victory over death and evil, must be proclaimed

23 Rev 17:5

and anchored. The blood of the martyrs testifies about this victory. When the young church asserted that Peter and Paul are forever present in Rome, it is the testimony of their blood for the greater glory of God in this city that the church had in mind.

12

One decisive question in regards to the primacy of the pope concerns the interpretation of the words in the gospel of Matthew's 16th chapter: "And I also say to you that you are Peter and on this rock I will build My church." Does Jesus mean that it is the *person* Peter that is the rock that He will build His church on? Or, is it the *confession* of Peter – "You are the Messiah, the Son of the living God." – that is the foundation upon which the church is built?

The majority of church fathers in the first centuries of the church, the Greek fathers of the east in particular, understood the "rock" to be the faith in Christ that Peter confessed in Caesarea Philippi. The church is founded on the rock, Christ. He is the truth, the foundation for the church and her faith. "In this regard, we are all heirs to Peter, personally as well as communally," writes Olivier Clément.

"If we also say to ourselves 'Thou art Christ, the Son of the living God,' then we too become Peter," wrote Origen" for whoever is united to Christ becomes Peter." In the same way, Augustine suggests "that it be understood as built upon Him who Peter confessed."

At the same time, the fathers recognized that the shepherds of the sheep carry a special responsibility for the church, built upon Christ, the Rock from where the life

giving water of the Holy Spirit flows. The church is not only built upon Christ as *Truth,* but also upon Christ as *Life*. Just like truth is conveyed to the church through the Word that is read and proclaimed, she receives the life of Christ primarily through the eucharist.

In the mother church of Jerusalem, it is Peter that proclaims the Word and breaks the bread in the place of Jesus when the Lord's table is celebrated. He is clothed in the *charismatic* garment that he had received from Jesus, not as the only one to receive this clothing but as the first among many.

13

Every single bishop, as well as the college of bishops (*episcopatus unus est*), sits on the chair of Peter (*Cathedra Petri),* Cyprian wrote in the 3rd century. In his text about the unity of the church, he suggests that the words of Jesus in Matthew 16 are the foundation for the episcopacy in the church. When Jesus speaks with Peter, "he gives the same authority to all the apostles," writes Cyprian.

What is valid for Peter is also valid for the twelve and therefore also for the bishops succeeding him by virtue of being heirs to Peter. Church fathers, particularly from the west, emphasized the connection between Peter's *person* and his *confession* as time went by. The rock is Peter as person by virtue of confessing the apostolic faith. As a consequence, another connection was put forward as time went by: the connection between the confession of Peter and the bishop of Rome as the first one of those who confessed this faith. This took a while, and historians cannot be certain that there was a monarchic episcopacy in Rome before

the second half of the 2nd century or if at this time there was only a college of presbyters and *episkopoi,* where some stood out more but without being consecrated bishops.

However, in the early 3rd century, the bishops of Rome began to reference Jesus's words in the gospel of Matthew, but even more the gospel of Luke 22:31-32 and the gospel of John 21:15-18, to galvanize the distinguished place they had as successors to Peter. The first to express this is Tertullian (not a bishop himself) when he wrote about the office of Peter in regard to unifying the bishops and guarding the unity of the church. The idea of that Peter received a special anointing from Jesus that made him the first among the apostles and that Rome's bishop is the successor of Peter, became more common at this time that.

At the same time, it was made very clear that Rome's leading position will never entail that the bishop of Rome has a judicial mandate over the other bishops. The Roman primacy "is one of confession, not of honor; of faith, not jurisdiction," writes Ambrose in the 4th century. The special anointing of the office of Peter is to guard the unity between the churches, to repel division that might arise and to intervene when called upon. The bishop of Rome was the successor of Peter after all, but his testimony needed to harmonize with that of Paul as well.

14

When the charismatic anointing of Peter eventually was written into canon law, it wasn't farfetched that the church in Rome with its bishop not only would become an obvious spiritual authority but also begin to lay hold of a juridical role in relation to the rest of the churches within Christianity.

Soon tensions arose. It was not easy to keep the balance and it required a bishop in Rome that was aware of his dependence on the synod of bishops. As long as Rome had bishops who incorporated the principle of the Roman bishop as *servus servorum Dei,* servant of the servants of God, one may consider the office of Peter as an office that served the unity of the church and exercised some prophetic charisma for the benefit and blessing of the Catholic Church.

One of the prime examples of this was the pontificate of Saint Gregory the Great in the beginning of the 7th century. He suggested that no bishop can speak about himself as "Catholic" if he does not submit to the other bishops. When Rome became subject to bishops who took advantage of their position, the office of Peter started to become a symbol of political power, with division and segregation as its consequence. The "pope," certainly from Protestant but also Orthodox perspectives eventually became synonymous with an unacceptable papacy.

15

Church structures and governing models that obscured the church from the foundational understanding of authority that we encounter in the gospels were developed over time. "But not so among you,"[24] Jesus said to His disciples when He rebuked their view on authority and their hunger for power. The church cannot be modeled after the absolute system of the Roman empire, the hierarchies of medieval society or contemporary democracy with decisions being made with majority vote.

24 Luke 22:26

The kingdom of heaven is a kingdom where power equals service, where *exousia* is translated with *diakonia.* The first shall be the last, *primate* becomes *kenosis.*[25] Jesus says, "All authority has been given Me."[26] The Father gives His authority to the Son, Who in turn gives it to the apostles by the power of the Holy Spirit. From the Father, to the Son, in the Holy Spirit: this is the pattern in the life of the Church.

Jesus also says, "I am with you always, even to the end of the age."[27] He is always present with the apostles even though He has given them His authority. He doesn't delegate His authority, He shares it. For this reason it becomes problematic to speak about a bishop as "the Vicar of Christ." A vicar or representative, by definition, represents someone who is not present. However, the risen Christ is very much present and does not need a representative. He is always and everywhere present through the Holy Spirit.

16

This brings us to a point that must never be overlooked when we discuss matters about authority within the church: *sensus fidelium,* the sense of the faithful. Through the outpouring of the Holy Spirit at Pentecost, the Holy Spirit is given to all who are baptized, not only a chosen few. The Holy Spirit speaks through the faithful. Through the events at Pentecost, everyone has become *charismatics* in the real sense of that word.

---

25 Exousia = authority, Diakonia = Service, Primate = First, Kenosis = self emptying/sacrifice Phil 2:7

26 Matt 28:18

27 Matt 28:20

To use the words of Simon Peter, all of us are a royal priesthood, a holy nation.[28] According to Paul, all who are baptized can prophesy.[29] Wherefore, Igantious of Laodicea, a more contemporary Orthodox Church leader writes, "The fellowship is the highest authority within the Church." Or, as expressed by Torsten Kälvemark, a lay theologian in the Orthodox Church, "The Church has only one leader: The Holy Spirit."

The tongues of fire that descended upon the disciples at Pentecost continue to descend upon the faithful. Therefore, John is able to write in his first letter, "But you have an anointing from the Holy One, and you know all things."[30] The personal pentecost of every Christian forms the foundation of the *sensus fidelium* of the church, her prophetic identity. This sense is more than an aloof sensation or a vague feeling; it is the voice of the Holy Spirit through God's people. It is a voice that on different occasions and in different seasons have corrected bishops and popes.

When the hierarchy in the church falls prey to hardness of heart or heresy there are people who are sent for the revival of the church by the Holy Spirit speaking to and through them. In this way, revivals have always been ignited throughout the history of the church. Movements like this have often been the expression of the gift of prophesy within the life of the church. They fulfill the words of Jesus: "However, when He, the Spirit of truth, has come, He will guide you into all truth."[31]

---

28 1 Pet 2:9
29 1 Cor 14:31
30 1 John 2:20
31 John 16:13

Nonetheless, the ones acting in a corrective way have not always been welcomed by the hierarchy of the church. The antagonism between the institutional and charismatic elements has always been a part of the church throughout her history. Through the prophets - the unavoidable tension that exists within Christianity between all forms of established institutions and the liberty of the Spirit is revealed, writes the Orthodox theologian John Meyendorff.

17

Can we understand Peter's call as a mission with a particular responsibility for the gift of truth, *charisma veritatis,* as a gift Jesus Himself gave to the apostles, who then passed it on to others? In a similar way, is Paul the archetype for the prophetic gift, standing up to face Peter? All of the faithful are the guardians of truth, but the bishop has a designated duty to proclaim and teach the Word of God in its fullness according to Paul's instruction to Timothy: "Be diligent to present yourself approved to God, a worker who does not need to be ashamed, rightly dividing the word of truth."[32]

However, when the leader fails, God appoints a prophet to correct the church. The authentic expression of the church in the world is revealed in this person. Olivier Clément adds a perspective based on the foundation of the gospel concerning this: when the personal conscience requires objection, "it must choose the way of martyrdom, not rebellion."

32 2 Tim 2:15

18

Many church leaders from both east and west relented to a heresy that arose in the 7th century. The so-called *monothelitism* consisted of the idea that Christ only had one will, the divine. The current bishop of Rome, Martin I, was so unrelenting in his opposition to this heresy that he was arrested by the emperor who sent soldiers to Rome to apprehend him, the pope himself. From there, Bishop Martin (the pope) was transferred in chains to Constantinople, where he was imprisoned, beaten and finally exiled to the Crimean peninsula where he died of exhaustion. He was replaced by a new, emperor-friendly pope in Rome.

Another who refused to relent was Maximos the Confessor, a monk and a layperson who remained faithful in a time of confusion and heresy in the church. When he was in exile, he was told by the emperor's messengers: "You are alone. The patriarch agrees. The pope of Rome agrees. You are outside the church."

"No," said Maximos. "If that is so, then I am the church." He suffered martyrdom for his confession of faith.

Hippolytus of Rome confirms this ability to discern and speak truth by individual persons when he wrote in the 3rd century, "With the Holy Spirit conferring perfect grace on those who have a correct faith, and so that they will know that those who are at the head of the Church must teach and guard all these things."

19

The question of the legitimacy concerning the office of Peter is and remains the decisive matter of conflict on the

journey toward the visible unity of the church. It concerns not only Protestant and Roman Catholics but also, to the same degree, Roman Catholics and Orthodox. As in any dialogue, it is necessary to begin with understanding the words we are using.

Is it legitimate – that is, in accordance with biblical and early Christian tradition – to even speak about the office of Peter? That depends on our interpretation. Can we agree that Peter received a particular call from Jesus? Can we also agree that this call, in a certain sense, extends to every overseer and bishop in the church since every local church is an expression of the fullness of the church? Can we agree that the primary mission of this person is to lay down his life to keep the unity in Christ, in the local congregation as well as in the fellowship with other churches? A mission that only can be fulfilled by a love for Christ.

If we are able to agree about these things, then dialogue concerning a common Christian understanding about the office of Peter may have a starting point. But, it gets trickier down the road. If any bishop or church claims ownership of this particular office it remains for them to incarnate this. This bishop must assume the greatest responsibility for the unity of the church by laying down his life for his brothers, just like Jesus and the apostles. Aligning with the words Jesus spoke to Peter, "Do you love Me more than these?"

20

It is in this light that Lewi Pethrus' letters provide a rare glimpse into the role that the farm boy from Vargön came to have as a church leader. The early Swedish Pentecostal movement was as far from a unified movement as you

could imagine. It consisted of endless channels and diversions, a host of disparate expressions, where the experience called "baptized in the Holy Spirit" was the one common denominator.

All across Sweden congregations were splintered of in this spiritual renewal. New constellations of congregations came into being, often finding themselves at the mercy of the ones with the loudest voice who felt called to lead.

There was much talk about miracles in the Pentecostal revival, but the greatest miracle, without a doubt, was that this multi-faceted spiritual movement held together. What was it that made the Pentecostal movement transform into a denominational one – a so-called church whose covenant and unity had few, if any, equivalents in other parts of the world where the Pentecostal movement had influence?

In this situation where tension and conflict was rampant, Lewi Pethrus (Peter in English) had an important role to play. To speak about the office of Peter is more that just a play on words. The unity that grew over time between the more than 500 congregations would have been impossible without the leadership of Lewi Pethrus. In reality, Pethrus came to function not only as a bishop like the ones during the time of Ignatius of Antioch, but more like how the bishop of Rome came to function in the early church. If the words "pope" or "bishop" hadn't developed a strong negative connotation in the Free Church movement, the words could have been used to accurately describe the function of Lewi Pethrus. He was a "father," which is the meaning of the word "pope," to all the congregations by mandate of being the pastor in the biggest and most prominent church in the Pentecostal movement, a "fatherhood" that found it's expression in the collegium of pastors. The office of

Peter was tied to the *charisma* and person of Lewi Pet For better or worse, this office never came to be institut alized within the Pentecostal movement. For better: hist testifies how an office like that so easily turns into a hunger for power and political maneuvering. For worse: without an office designated for the unity in a church or congregation, it becomes hard to protect this unity from divisive and emotional tendencies as time goes by. The history of Protestantism painfully demonstrates this.

21

"The miracle of unity has already begun." These words were spoken by the current bishop of Rome, Pope Francis, who has surprised many people drawn to the Roman Catholic Church by emphatically encouraging them to function as bridge-builders where they currently find themselves rather than converting to the Roman Catholic Church. As he told a Protestant leader recently, "I'm not interested in converting Evangelicals to Catholicism. I want people to find Jesus in their own community."

When knots are untied, many things can happen in a short timeframe. To use one example, the Pope is convinced that the Reformation is over. It came to an end in 1999. That year, the Roman Catholic Church and the Lutheran World Federation agreed upon a joint declaration concerning the justification through faith – the point of doctrine that formed the heart of Luther's protest. When the two churches, after long and deliberate conversations, concluded that there was a shared understanding between them concerning "justification by grace through faith in Christ," the Reformation came to an end. In 2006

this declaration was accepted by the worldwide Methodist Church as well.

Evangelical and protestant Christians may not even be aware that the Reformation is over. In just a few years, this pope has removed obstacles for unity that have been built up for decades. He has visited Pentecostals in the south of Italy as well as Waldensians up in the northern parts of the country. As the prime representative of the Roman Catholic Church, he has asked forgiveness for how his church has treated fellow brothers and sisters within other parts of Christianity.

In the spirit of the pope, more and more people are speaking about "convergence" rather than "converting," a mutual movement toward each other, with respect and a shared humility, without attitudes of indignation or triumphalism. In that place, wounds can be healed and mistrust can be overcome. The key to unity is spelled *collegiality,* not supremacy, for the sake of the spirit of the gospel and the spreading of the same. Engaging the work of unity can "not be about diplomacy or forced submission any longer, it is the necessary way of evangelization," the current bishop of Rome suggests. This requires bravery and, first and foremost, an openness to the Holy Spirit.

As Pope Francis expresses it, "If we really believe in the abundantly free working of the Holy Spirit, we can learn so much from one another! It is not just about being better informed about others, but rather reaping what the Spirit has sown in them, which is also meant to be a gift for us." Sooner than we know, we may witness how believers from different denominations converge around the Lord's table because, in a mutual spirit of humility, we recognize the different gifts in the church that by definition can never be other than *One.*

A word from the translator

Translation is ecumenical in nature. Ever since the curse of Babel, when the common tongue was disrupted by God, translations of our subsequent languages has been a necessity for communication to occur. Communication, which literally means "communion under way" is indeed the prerequisite for communion for how can we have communion worth its salt without getting to know each other?

It is because of this reason that I felt compelled to translate this short but valuable book. It is not very often that a book of this format manages to touch upon the nature of the Church and her ecumenical mandate in a comprehensive yet accessible way. Peter Halldorf manages to do this, incorporating the tones and nuances of both Reformed, Roman and Orthodox Traditions. Without hesitation, he boldly stands in his own Pentecostal tradition, while embracing the gifts of other traditions. A feat that is only possible by leading a life of prayer and seeking the face of Jesus Christ, by the power of the Holy Spirit.

I personally identify with Peter Halldorf because I was raised, and am now a priest, in the Evangelical Orthodox Church. These two words, Evangelical and Orthodox are

contradictory according to many. If we understand them as political words, designating certain groups of people, I would tend to agree. But if we understand them in a different light, then we realize that an Orthodox faith is Evangelical and an Evangelical faith is Orthodox. Just as Catholic faith is Pentecostal and a Pentecostal faith is Catholic. Behind all the man-made labels, there is still only one Church.

Translation, as well as ecumenism, is about transmitting this true Spirit of the heart and for that to happen we need to restore and rejuvenate our relationships. We need to find ourselves going beyond the words.

As we begin to translate, as we begin to try to understand the intended meaning, we more often than not begin to transform as well, we "rub off" on each other, and maybe that is what the Lord intended? If we submit to each other in love, I am sure that the ecumenical process, the process of knowing the other while remaining who you are, can begin either at the pulpit or the altar.

I am glad that this ecumenical book, originally written in Swedish, is now translated into English. Not because there is a lack of very good ecumenical books in English but because it is a sign of that the

Holy Spirit is still at work in the Church. Although written with a Swedish framework in mind, it is my hope that you have been able to pick up the thoughts that can be applied to any context. In that way, the very act of reading this translation becomes a part of the answer to Jesus own prayer, *that they may be one.*

Jakob Palm
Holy Covenant Evangelical Orthodox Church
Saskatoon

Bibliography

Andrén, Olof och Beskow, Per (red): De apostoliska fäderna. (The apostolic fathers) Artos, 2006.

Brodd, Sven-Erik, Tjørhom, Ola: Protestantismen eller katolicitet? Om kyrkans väsen i en ekumenisk tid. (Protestantism or catholicity? The essence of the church in a time of ecumenism) Artos, 2001.

Clément, Olivier: You are Peter. An Orthodox Theologian's Reflection on the Exercise of Papal Primacy. New City Press, 2003.

Halldorf, Joel: Lewis brev (The letters of Lewi) Libris, 2007.

Matta al-Miskin: Enhet ger liv. (Unity gives life) Silentium skrifter, 2000.

Pope Francis: Evangeliets glädje. (The Joy of the Gospel) Veritas förlag, 2014.

Vallquist, Gunnel: Vad väntar vi egentligen på? (What are we waiting for?) Cordia, 2002.

About the author

Peter Halldorf is a pastor in the Pentecostal movement in Sweden. He is involved with the ecumenical community and retreat centre Bjärka-Säby near Linköping, Sweden. He is the chief editor and publisher of the ecumenical periodical *Pilgrim,* as well as the author of twenty-nine books.

http://tidskriftenpilgrim.ekibs.se

About the translator

Jakob Palm is a priest in the Evangelical Orthodox Church. Born and raised in Sweden, he moved to Canada to pursue his vocation. He lives with his wife Ashley and son Elias in Saskatoon. He is involved with the ecumenical work in the city.

www.evangelicalorthodox.org

Made in United States
Troutdale, OR
01/17/2025